I0759552

HOW DOES YOUR GARDEN GROW?

The elements of planning, growing & caring for a garden

MILLI PROUST

Photography by Éva Németh

Quadrille

For my sister Imogen

This book is for you, to answer every gardening question you've ever asked me. Your curiosity, patience and endless enthusiasm shaped these pages more than you know. Thank you for reading, questioning, proofing and pushing me to make it better. I couldn't have done it without you.

A selection of sweet peas: 'Theia-Bella', 'Suzy Z', 'Windsor' with bronze fennel behind

GARDENER (FATHER)

It's a long way down the garden:
the lawn, the winding path through shrubs
The orchard, the kitchen bit –
a few bean stalks blackened by frost
only half the patch dug over –
and now, hidden by brambles;
I find his potting shed. I break a web
as I enter – it is dusty, damp,
on the floor are flower pots and broken crocks
and rusty-lidded creosote.
There's order too: tools hang on pegs,
seed packets, dibbers, old bone labels
lie on the bench, and underneath
are piles of yellowed newspapers
dated nineteen sixty-eight.
Your Harris tweed, elbow-patched,
hangs on the door. In its pockets
matches, pipe, Gold Flake baccy tin,
and a crumpled note: *replace glass,*
(twelve and a half inches by ten).
I look up at the window
its corners are festooned
with shrouds of bees and flies
I can see the prints of your thumb
in the putty round one pane.

by Jane Shelton (GJ, my grandmother)

CONTENTS

INTRODUCTION

Why I Garden

Time passes differently in a garden. It's not rushed, not sharp-edged or finite like it so often feels elsewhere. Instead, it unspools in petals and seed pods, in soft changes and quiet returns. I think that's why I love it. The slow, faithful rhythm of the year allows me to think differently about time; it's not measured by a clock, but by the natural cycle of all things. The first crocus cracks open the year. Then come the tulips, the foxgloves, the bees, the soft summer evenings. By the time the leaves start to fall, I can feel it in my bones, the shape of another year lived in flowers. As I write this, overlooking the winter garden glistening with ice, I can't help but marvel at the fact that I've been tending to this plot for ten years. A fact that still surprises me, mostly when I find myself battling weeds taller than me, or realising I've planted something entirely wrong. Again.

Stepping into the garden can feel like stepping into a conversation between me, the land, the weather, the plants, and all the people who grew before me. Every time I tuck a seed into the soil, I feel more connected, more rooted. In the garden I find a place where griefs and torments can be buried, and sometimes something beautiful emerges. Except when the beauty that emerges is bindweed. I really struggle with bindweed. But even then, gardening holds everything; creation, identity, renewal, humility. Through the act of tending and enjoying, I'm constantly reminded of the chance the land gives to begin again. To just keep trying. Growing isn't just about beauty or food or even joy. It's about remembering that we're not separate from nature, we're part of it.

Gardening is more than just growing things; it is a personal journey for each of us who do it, and in many ways, an act of legacy. An unbroken thread that ties us to the countless growers who came before us, each other, and those yet to come. I often think about how seeds and knowledge, once shared around kitchen tables or at the edge of fields, have travelled across centuries and continents to end up in our hands today. It's seeds that have really fuelled my obsession with gardening, that spark of possibility that lives inside something so small gets me every time. The techniques we use to sow, the plants we grow,

and the lessons we learn along the way, are all echoes of a past where tending the earth was not just a necessity but an act of community, resilience and care. I like to think that I can feel that all in the bliss of working in the borders.

In a garden, we become both stewards and creators, inheritors and innovators. Gardening asks us to carry forward with care, to move towards the future while honouring what came before. Seeds, cuttings, and plants all hold the past, present, and future within them. They carry the wisdom of centuries, from those who first cultivated the land, to those who coaxed wild plants into food and medicine, and to those who grew not only for sustenance, but for delight and wonder. When we pass down plant knowledge, whether through books, conversations or the simple act of giving someone a cutting or a packet of seeds, we're keeping something alive that's bigger than any one garden.

When I first arrived here in West Sussex and suddenly became custodian of a garden, I felt completely unprepared. My previous growing had been limited to a few pots and window boxes, dragged from flat-share to flat-share. They were a mix of triumphs (sweet peas spilling over the edges) and disasters (everything else). But there was enough magic in those pots to keep me going, to keep me dreaming, and they eventually led me here, to this piece of land that changed the course of my life. This garden became a place of solace, somewhere to work through life's peaks and troughs, to focus my energy, to clear my mind, and to bury the parts of myself I no longer needed. It's also been a place of joy and connection, where friends and family gather, where life hums and unfolds against a backdrop of beauty.

I love being a gardener. I'm not a designer or a horticultural expert, just a gardener who has built a space I cherish. It's not perfect (ask me about the time I accidentally grew the world's tallest teasel here*), but as I prepare to move on and pass this garden to someone new, I can say without hesitation: I have loved every messy, magical corner of it. A good garden, like life, evolves and grows with us. This one has felt alive, full of whimsy and charm, a good blend of productivity and beauty. And now, after a decade of loving this space, I want to share how I shaped it, not because it's flawless, but because it's been real. I hope it offers a little guidance, a little encouragement, and a nudge to help you build the garden of your dreams too.

Nellie Brant x

*At the time of writing I have the Guinness World Record for the Tallest Teasel. Really. Truly. It's 3.98m (13ft).

HOW TO USE THIS BOOK

This book is intended to feel like a conversation between friends over a cup of tea, you and I looking over your space and scribbling ideas, a companion to guide you through the small steps it takes to grow and care for your dream garden. You can read it cover to cover or jump to the sections that address your needs in the moment.

The chapters cover the essentials of understanding, starting and designing a garden. You'll learn how to plan your space, calculate how many plants you'll need and choose ideal varieties for year-round interest. There's guidance on caring for your garden and practical advice on propagating plants at little to no cost. Seasonal tasks, personal stories, and lessons I learned are woven throughout the book. A detailed glossary at the very back demystifies unfamiliar terms.

Nasturtium 'Bloody Mary'

STARTING A GARDEN

The first time I sat in this garden, it felt as though the plants could see how little I knew. Faced with the daunting task of figuring out where to start, I was overwhelmed. My urge to garden was intense, but my knowledge was nonexistent. How do you configure a garden? What do you plant, and where and why? The sheer number of questions made me want to go lie down, and preferably somewhere without weeds.

It's been one steep learning curve since then, and while there have been moments of great elation, there have also been moments when I wanted to shout, 'What is wrong with this plant?' only to realize, begrudgingly, that the plant wasn't the problem. Starting anything new can be intimidating, but here's the good news: you don't need to panic. I'm here to help break it all down into manageable steps.

There are four key pieces of advice I wish someone had shared with me at the start. These concepts are good to keep in mind whether you're beginning from scratch or thinking about what fresh ideas you can bring to a mature garden.

First, **there isn't a time limit.** You don't have to do everything at once. A garden isn't like a reality TV makeover with a dramatic reveal. It's more like a symphony, unfolding slowly, in movements. Some plants arrive like a bright fanfare, others linger in the background, building quietly over time. Each season brings a shift in rhythm, a new theme, a variation on the last. Gardens take time to mature, and that's part of their beauty. Ten years into tending this space, I'm still learning, adjusting and occasionally tripping over my mistakes. The work of a garden is never done, and that's where the magic lives. There's life, death, movement, mud and plenty of beauty in between.

Second, **you can start at any time of year.** There's no such thing as 'gardening season' because the rhythm of a garden is a continuous cycle. Summer offers inspiration, autumn invites action, winter gives you space to dream, and spring bursts with energy. No matter what time of year it is, there's always something you can do, even if it's just sitting and imagining the possibilities.

Third, **right plant, right place.** This golden rule of gardening, popularized by the legendary gardener Beth Chatto, is like finding your plant's forever home. It's all about matching plants to the environment they'll thrive in. Think of a sunny border filled with cheerful perennials such as achillea (a personal favourite) and salvias (perfect under roses). Contrast that with the shady, cool charm of a woodland garden, where hellebores, dicentras and heucheras shine with their delicate blooms and striking foliage. By choosing plants suited to their environment, you're not just creating a healthier garden, you're working harmoniously with nature and reducing resource use (see more on page 75 and 77–83).

Finally, **leave and watch or dive right in?** Ah, the eternal question. The temptation to dive headfirst into pulling out, designing, and replanting can be oh-so-strong – trust me, I've been there, wide-eyed at a plant nursery, filling my arms with things I couldn't even pronounce. But there's wisdom in observing your garden for a year. Watch how the light shifts, note what plants already thrive and see how wildlife interacts with the space. If you have the luxury of time, this patience can help you create a more thoughtful, harmonious garden. That said, if your gardening space is temporary or you're itching to get your hands dirty, there's nothing wrong with diving in – just know that mistakes are part of the process.

Gardens, like people, are always evolving. You'll make mistakes, learn lessons and uncover hidden joys along the way. Remember, this isn't about creating perfection. It's about creating a space that grows with you – a space that reflects your unique blend of hope and creativity, plus a fair amount of trial and error.

THE ESSENTIALS

PLANT TYPES

Plants can be grouped into different categories based on their lifecycle and growing conditions. Understanding these classifications helps you choose the right plants for your garden and manage them throughout the seasons.

ANNUALS

Plants that complete their entire lifecycle – germinating, growing, flowering and setting seed – within one growing season are known as annuals. Once their seeds are produced, the plants naturally die back. In short, if you get an annual plant, it will not be returning, unless it self-seeds or you save the seed and sow it the following year.

Tender annuals: These annuals love the heat and need warmth to thrive. They cannot stand winter's cold and wet conditions. They're particularly vulnerable to frost. They need warm soil and air to germinate and grow well, making them ideal for summer planting. **Examples:** celosia, marigold, zinnia.

Half-hardy annuals: These annuals shy away from cold. They are vulnerable to a hard frost, so they're best started under cover. **Examples:** cobaea, cosmos, nasturtium, nicotiana, snapdragon, stock.

Hardy annuals: Tougher than their tender counterparts, hardy annuals can tolerate cold weather. These plants thrive in the ground rather than containers and can even be planted in autumn to bloom the following early summer. Sowing them in modules in autumn and overwintering them under cover is another great option. They can also be sown in spring for later blooms. **Examples:** ammi, calendula, cerinthe, cornflower, nigella, sweet pea, wild carrot.

BIENNIALS

Biennials follow a two-year cycle. In the first year, they germinate and grow foliage. After a cold period (vernalization), they flower and set seed (usually in the second year). Once they have set seed, they have completed their lifecycle and die. Sow these plants in early summer to enjoy their blooms the following late spring or early summer. **Examples:** angelica, dianthus, foxglove, hollyhock, Icelandic poppy, sweet rocket.

PERENNIALS

Plants that live for more than two years, returning season after season, are known as perennials. Depending on the type, they can offer long-lasting beauty and structure.

Short-lived perennials: Not all perennials are built to last forever. Some will live for only three to five years before fading away. **Examples:** aquilegia, lupin.

Herbaceous perennials: These perennials are non-woody plants that die back to the ground at the end of the growing season. In spring, they send up fresh new shoots, ready to bloom again. **Examples:** achillea, delphinium, nepeta, salvia, sanguisorba, sea holly.

PERENNIALS TREATED AS ANNUALS

Some plants that are technically perennials behave like annuals in cooler climates, flowering in one growing season. However, in their native or warmer climates, they can overwinter and perform better in subsequent years. **Examples:** amaranth, coneflower, rudbeckia.

SHRUBS

Shrubs are woody plants that are smaller than trees and have multiple stems. With their permanent framework of branches, shrubs provide year-round interest and structure in the garden. They can be evergreen or deciduous. **Examples:** choisya, forsythia, hydrangea, lilac, nandina, rose, witch hazel.

TREES

The giants of the plant world, trees have elongated woody stems or trunks that can grow in multiples or singularly. These perennial plants are essential for ecosystems, providing oxygen, improving air quality and offering habitat for wildlife. **Examples:** apple, beech, cherry, hazel, maple, oak.

BULBS

The underground storage bud of a plant that contains everything a plant needs to grow and flower. **Examples:** allium, daffodil, tulip.

CLIMBERS

Plants that grow vertically, grabbing onto walls, trellises or fences. They're perfect to add height and softening hardscapes. **Examples:** clematis, jasmine, wisteria.

Rose 'Roald Dahl' and common foxgloves (*Digitalis purpurea* and *Digitalis purpurea f. albiflora*)

A GARDENER'S ESSENTIAL TOOLS

Tools that earn their keep, season after season

Every gardener, whether a novice or seasoned expert, benefits from having the right tools. A well-rounded toolkit not only makes gardening more efficient but also more enjoyable. Each tool has a specific role to play, helping to make tasks more manageable. There's no need to buy the entire garden shed right away – choose tools according to your current projects and collect them over time.

You don't need to splurge on new tools immediately. Plenty of perfectly good second-hand tools can be sourced through online auction sites, second-hand shops and local networks. Garden centres, hardware stores and online retailers also offer a wide variety of new tools to suit any budget. Keep your tools in good repair (see page 196) and they will last for years.

Trug with hand fork, trowel, secateurs, dibbers, and hori hori

BASIC GARDEN TOOLKIT

TROWEL

A trowel is indispensable for planting and bulb placement. Its small, handheld design allows precise digging in tight spaces, making it perfect for borders, pots and raised beds. Opt for one with a sturdy, ergonomic handle and a rust-resistant blade for durability.

HAND FORK OR HORI HORI KNIFE

Both tools excel at loosening compacted soil and tackling weeds, but the hori hori knife takes versatility to another level. With its serrated edge, it's ideal for cutting through roots, slicing into the soil for bulbs or seedlings, and thanks to its built-in gradations, even measuring planting depths. I find it to be a truly multifunctional must-have.

SECATEURS

High-quality secateurs are vital for pruning, deadheading and shaping plants.

Bypass secateurs: *(where the upper blade slices past the lower blade) Great for clean, precise cuts on live stems.*

Anvil secateurs: *(where the two blades meet, creating a forceful, sharp crushing action) Used for tougher deadwood trimming.*

LOPPERS

For cutting back thicker branches or shaping shrubs, loppers provide extra reach and power. Look for a lightweight yet strong pair with adjustable handles for tackling both fine and heavy pruning tasks.

GLOVES

Protective gloves are a gardener's best friend, shielding hands from thorns and dirt, and preventing blisters. Choose durable, flexible gloves suited to the task at hand – thorn-resistant gloves for pruning and lighter gloves for delicate planting.

RAKE

A rake is perfect for levelling soil in newly prepared beds, gathering leaves or clearing debris. Consider a soil rake for fine levelling and a leaf rake for broader clean-up tasks.

SPADE

A spade, with its flat, sharp-edged blade, is essential for digging, edging and cutting through tough roots. Invest in one with a long, sturdy handle and a comfortable grip for efficient digging with less strain.

HOE

Ideal for weeding and soil preparation, the hoe excels at removing surface weeds and breaking up clumpy soil to create a finer tilth for planting. Different types, such as draw hoes and Dutch hoes, are tailored to specific weeding and cultivating needs.

Draw hoe: *Typically a sharp angled blade. Great for pulling soil towards you, slicing weeds and creating furrows.*

Dutch hoe: *Typically a stirrup shape to be used in a push-pull action. Used for slicing weeds just below the soil's surface.*

WHEELBARROW

A sturdy wheelbarrow is invaluable for transporting soil, compost, plants and tools. For smaller gardens, consider a lightweight barrow; for larger spaces, a heavy-duty model can handle bulkier loads with ease. I highly recommend choosing one with a solid ball wheel instead of an inflatable one if possible as wheelbarrow punctures can be a pain to deal with – it is worth holding out for a good one that won't need much maintenance.

WATERING CAN AND HOSE

Both tools are essential for efficient irrigation. A watering can with a detachable rose head is perfect for gentle watering of seedlings, while a hose with an adjustable nozzle allows for versatile coverage.

TRUG

A trug is a lightweight, portable basket for collecting weeds, debris or harvested produce. It's also great for carrying hand tools.

ALMA | PROUST
ALMA | PROUST
SILENE DIOICA
ALMA | PROUST
ZINNIA

SEED-STARTING TOOLS

PRICKING-OUT TOOL

This is very handy if you plan to be growing from seed. While your finger can suffice for making a small planting hole, a specialized pricking-out tool makes transplanting seedlings far easier. A fine-pointed tool, such as a sneeboer (see page 154), helps gently lift seedlings without damaging delicate roots, ensuring better survival rates during transplantation.

BUTTER KNIFE

A butter knife (with a round-tip blade) is the perfect tool for sliding seedlings out of pots and tray cells.

POTS

My favourite to use are 9-cm (4-inch) pots, I find them versatile for many sized seedlings. These are indispensable for growing plants from seeds and cuttings, or for housing tender plants. Choose a mix of sizes to accommodate various stages of plant development, and ensure they have proper drainage holes for healthy root growth. A pot can be anything that can hold soil and allow water to flow through freely. A great space-saving alternative are pot slips, which are essentially pots that fold flat.

SEED TRAYS

My preferred seed trays are: quarter sized (9.5 x 15.5 cm/4 x 6 inches), half sized (19 x 22 cm/ 7 x 9 inches), and a plug tray with 77 cells (35 x 50 cm/14 x 20 inches). These trays hold soil for starting seeds in an organized way, making it easier to manage and monitor germination. They are particularly useful for growing a large number of seedlings in a small space (see page 148).

PROPAGATING LIDS

These are clear plastic covers placed over seed trays or pots to create a warm, humid environment that promotes germination and protects young seedlings from draughts and temperature fluctuations. They're useful for starting seeds indoors or in greenhouses, and helpful to protect freshly sown seeds from being nibbled by pests.

WATER TRAYS

If you add water to these trays and place them underneath seed trays or pots, they allow plants to draw water up from the tray, keeping the soil moist without disturbing the seeds or seedlings. This is known as bottom watering.

PLANT LABELS

These blank stick labels help you keep track of what you've sown or planted, especially when working with multiple varieties. Write clearly and use durable labels to withstand weathering. You can use a little nail polish remover to clean off last season's writing and make it reusable.

GARDEN PEN

I've had a few sorry seasons where my annotations on the plant labels faded quickly, leaving me unsure of what was what. Unlike permanent markers, a garden pen is made to write on plant labels and resist weather conditions, such as rain and sunlight, so it won't smudge or fade.

GETTING THE BEST FROM YOUR PLOT

To get the best out of your garden, you'll need to build up a detailed picture of the plot. It starts with the soil, holding it in your hands and working out its composition. Next is light, where it falls, at what time of day, and how that shifts and changes throughout the year. Then water, because noting where the wet and dry spots are is really important. Finally, the nature you have, seeing what is growing and thriving where, what sorts of weeds you have, and how the wildlife uses them. Over the next few sections, I'll share information on each of these elements, hopefully equipping you with the knowledge to study your space, as well as a few pointers on choosing the plants that will flourish within it.

Rose 'Roald Dahl' and common foxgloves

LEARNING YOUR PLOT

The most important and basic elements to learn about in your garden are **Soil**, **Light** and **Water.** These three elements are the most critical components of a plant's life essentials.

In the planning stage of a garden, understanding and learning about these elements specific to your space is crucial. It will dictate what plants you can choose to bring into the space, ensuring that you will have the happiest and healthiest garden.

Knowing the space you have to work with is a helpful way of avoiding time-consuming and costly mistakes when starting a garden from scratch or doing a garden overhaul. I've spent a lot of time, energy and money trying to grow bearded iris in the heavy clay soil in my garden. On reflection, I could have simply grown them in pots and embraced the winter-wet-loving plants in the ground instead – this would have saved a lot of heartache. Having a greater understanding of your garden, its conditions, and strengths and limitations will help you make choices that are in tune with your soil, aspect and climate, helping you build a garden that will thrive and be beautiful.

So how do we do this? How do we actively engage in the process of learning our space? Discovering the idiosyncrasies of the land has been one of my favourite and most rewarding parts of creating my garden. Try the following exercises.

TAKE PICTURES

Make it a habit to photograph your garden regularly, ideally every week or at least once a month. Jot down notes about any new plant arrivals – where they appear, when they emerge and how long they last. This simple practice helps to track growth patterns and seasonal changes, giving you valuable insight into your garden.

WATCH WHAT'S GROWING WHERE

If you're working with an existing garden, take time to observe what's already thriving. If possible, spend a full year identifying plants and noting their conditions. This will provide clues about your garden's soil, light and moisture levels, as well as helping you to decide what you like or don't like about the current layout. For support, try using one of the many plant identification apps available or use a plant encyclopedia.

Malus 'Royalty', *Physocarpus* 'Amber Queen' and Cosmos 'Xanthos'

OBSERVE THE ELEMENTS

Stand in your garden and notice how natural elements interact with the space.

Wind: Note where it hits the hardest and how strong it is on both calm and windy days.

Frost: Observe where frost lingers longest and where it thaws first.

Sunlight: Track how sunlight moves through your garden at different times of the day and year.

Moisture: Identify areas that stay wet or dry and where water naturally pools.

These observations will help you to identify microclimates – areas with unique conditions, such as full sun, partial shade or specific moisture levels. Use these microclimates to guide your plant choices and create comfortable spaces for sitting, eating and enjoying your garden.

FEEL IT OUT

Pay attention to how your home or surrounding buildings relate to your garden. Notice how they influence light and shade, and identify spaces where you feel exposed or overlooked. Look for spots you're naturally drawn to for sitting or spending time, and use these insights to guide your design choices.

LOOK AT THE SOIL

Assess your soil across different areas of your garden, not just in one spot. Soil conditions can vary widely, and understanding these differences will save you time and money by helping you choose plants that thrive in your specific environment. For more on analyzing soil type and promoting soil health, see pages 23–5.

Dig into the soil: Dig a small hole to gauge the depth of your topsoil. This will help you to understand your garden's growing conditions and choose the right plants for each area (see page 24 and 77).

Test the pH: Conduct a pH test on your soil (see page 23).

SOIL

The foundation of your garden

Soil is where it all begins – it's the lifeblood of your garden and at the heart of nearly all plant life. It provides your plants with the essentials: oxygen, water and nutrients. The better your soil delivers these three necessities, the healthier and happier your garden will be.

But even if you're dealing with challenging soil conditions, you can still create a garden that's both beautiful and thriving. Many plants have evolved to flourish with less water, fewer nutrients and less oxygen, and giving them too much of these elements can sometimes do more harm than good. The key is understanding your soil and working with it to create a garden that suits your space and its unique conditions.

SOIL PH AND TYPE

WHY IT MATTERS

The acidity and alkalinity of soil, referred to as its pH levels, varies from one soil type to another. Both soil type and pH determine which nutrients are available to plants, influencing their ability to thrive. For example, dogwood (*Cornus*) and astilbe flourish in moisture-retentive clay soils, while lavender and thyme prefer well-drained, sandy soils, where nutrients drain quickly. Similarly, ericaceous plants, such as rhododendrons and blueberries, thrive in acidic soils but struggle in alkaline conditions, where plants such as clematis and sedum excel.

Getting to know your soil is essential, it helps you to choose plants that will thrive and ensures your garden is less work and more joy. Start by identifying two things:

- Soil type
- Soil pH

SOIL TYPES

Certain plants will thrive in different soil conditions and fail in others. It's far easier to work with your soil type in your plant choices than to battle against it; your garden will be healthier and happier for it, and growing will be much less hard work.

Chalk: Stony, free-draining and often alkaline. Shallow chalk soils are prone to drought, while deeper chalk can support more plants.

Sand: Gritty and free-draining but struggles to retain moisture and nutrients. It's well-aerated and warms quickly, making it ideal for drought-tolerant plants.

Clay: Dense and sticky, clay holds nutrients well but drains slowly. It stays cool in spring, which can delay growth, but it's excellent for moisture-loving plants.

Silt: Rare and highly fertile, silt soil has fine particles that can compact easily. It's often found near rivers and may require care to prevent erosion.

Loam: A balanced mix of sand, silt and clay, loam is the dream soil – crumbly, nutrient-rich and well-draining. Loam is highly desired by gardeners because it makes for good plant growth. In addition, it supports a wide range of plants, from vegetables and flowers to shrubs and trees.

Heavy clay soil

HOW TO TEST YOUR SOIL TYPE

Roll a ball of damp soil in your hand, then examine it.

Chalk: Tends to be gritty and may not form a ball. It often breaks apart easily due to its free-draining nature.

Sand: Crumbles almost immediately and does not hold together well.

Loam: Will hold together lightly when formed into a ball, but it will crumble under pressure.

Clay: Forms a firm ball that holds its shape due to its cohesive properties.

Silt: Holds together in a sticky, smooth ball but is more prone to compaction than loam, offering a distinct slippery feel when compared to the other types.

As you add organic matter over the years, your soil will evolve, becoming more balanced and loamy. Regularly checking its texture helps you monitor these changes and adjust your gardening approach as needed.

SOIL PH

Your soil's pH determines which nutrients are soluble and available to your plants. Most plants thrive in neutral soil (pH 6.0–7.0), but plenty of species have adapted to acidic or alkaline environments. For example, rhododendrons love acidic soils, while lavender and rosemary prefer more alkaline conditions.

HOW TO TEST YOUR SOIL'S PH

- Observe the types of plants growing naturally in your area.
- Use an at-home soil testing kit or send a sample for professional analysis.

Once you know your soil's pH, you can embrace plants suited to it or make gentle amendments. For long-lived perennials, shrubs and trees, matching plants to your soil is particularly important. Annuals, being temporary residents, are more forgiving and can be used to fill in gaps.

In some cases, you can work backwards by observing which plants are thriving in your garden and making a guess about the soil's pH.

Mophead hydrangeas and lacecap hydrangeas both act as visual pH indicators because their flowers turn blue in acidic soils and pink in alkaline soils.

Rhododendrons, camellias, heathers and azaleas: Thrive in acidic soils. Their healthy growth can indicate soil with a lower pH.

Lupins: Prefer acidic soil, making their success a potential pH indicator.

Clematis: Often does well in alkaline or neutral soils, hinting at a higher pH if it's thriving.

Lilacs: Favour alkaline or neutral soil and can struggle in acidic conditions, providing a clue to higher pH levels.

SOIL HEALTH

Healthy soil teems with life beneath your feet. From microbes to earthworms, everything works together to support your plants. These organisms decompose organic matter, release nutrients and improve soil structure.

SIGNS OF HEALTHY SOIL

Earthworm activity: A thriving population of earthworms indicates well-aerated, nutrient-rich soil. Look for earthworm tunnels or spot them during digging, these natural soil conditioners work to mix and improve your garden's earth.

Pleasant earthy smell: Soil with a balanced microbial population smells fresh and earthy, not sour or musty.

Good drainage: Water should soak in easily without pooling or running off too quickly. Pooling can be a sign of compaction (see below).

Abundant organic matter: Visible decomposed material, such as bits of leaves or compost, signals a nutrient-rich environment for plants.

Vigorous plant growth: Healthy soil results in lush, vibrant plants with strong roots, healthy leaves and steady growth.

SIGNS OF UNHEALTHY SOIL

Compaction: If the soil feels like it's hard and dense, it could be restricting root growth and impeding water infiltration.

Poor plant health: Symptoms such as yellowing leaves, stunted growth or wilting, despite adequate watering, may indicate nutrient deficiencies or pH imbalances in the soil. These issues often stem from a lack of essential nutrients or improper soil conditions that hinder plant development.

MICROBES: THE UNSUNG HEROES

Microbes, such as bacteria and fungi, decompose organic material, recycle nutrients and promote plant growth. They thrive in well-aerated soil with plenty of organic matter.

Threats to microbes

- Soil compaction from heavy machinery or rain.
- Poor drainage or excessive wetness in clay soils.
- Extreme pH levels (too acidic or too alkaline).

EARTHWORMS: THE SOIL'S ENGINEERS

Earthworms are nature's soil improvers, drawing organic matter into the earth, aerating it and mixing in nutrients. They bring mineral-rich subsoil to the surface, creating a fertile environment for plant roots.

How to support earthworms

- Avoid chemical fertilizers and pesticides.
- Add organic matter, such as compost or mulch.
- Leave the soil undisturbed as much as possible.

Worm-friendly practices

- If you want to use fertilizer, choose a natural one, such as compost and comfrey tea (see page 204), or seaweed extract.
- Mulch with organic materials to maintain moisture and temperature (see page 50).
- Minimize digging to preserve the soil's structure and ecosystem.

HOW TO NURTURE HEALTHY SOIL

Every garden faces its own challenges, but the best gardens embrace their soil's unique qualities. For example, heavy clay may not suit grasses for a prairie-style garden but will support nutrient-loving roses beautifully. Sandy soil, while quick-draining, creates the perfect home for drought-tolerant plants such as bearded iris and bronze fennel.

One of the best lessons that my garden has taught me is to embrace the soil type, and not to worry if it's not the much-desired loam. Whether you're dealing with chalk, sand or sticky clay, there are plants that will love your space as much as you do. Gardening is all about finding that balance, and when your soil is healthy, your plants will be too.

- *Add organic matter regularly (compost, manure or leaf mould).*
- *Minimize disturbance by avoiding unnecessary digging.*
- *Test your soil annually to monitor pH and nutrient levels (see page 24).*
- *Mulch to retain moisture and regulate soil temperature.*

WATER

The key to balanced, thriving plants

Water is one of the most important factors in gardening, and understanding how it moves through your plot can make all the difference. By embracing the natural conditions of your garden, you can create a space that uses fewer resources, and is both more sustainable and beautiful. Though it can be a bit harder to track water in your garden, as opposed to something like sunlight or frost, it is still a useful exercise in the observation of your space.

These observations will help you understand where the soil is draining and where it is holding water. Recognizing these patterns is the first step. The information in this section should inform your understanding of your garden's natural drainage, so you can choose the right plants for the right places.

Fritillaria meleagris (snakeshead frittilary), which flourishes in areas where water lingers

OBSERVING WATER IN YOUR SPACE

Take a moment to observe your garden during and after rainfall.

- *Are there spots where water pools after rain, lingering on the surface instead of draining away?*
- *Are there areas where water never seems to reach, leaving the soil dry even after several rainy days?*

These observations will help you understand where the soil is draining and where it is holding water. Recognizing these patterns is the first step in creating a garden that thrives. The information in this section should inform your understanding of your garden's natural drainage, so you can choose the right plants for the right places.

However, even plants within the same family can have vastly different moisture needs. Matching plants to their preferred moisture levels not only ensures their success but also simplifies your work as a gardener. Take the fritillary, for example:

- Bog-loving *Fritillaria meleagris* (pictured left) will flourish in areas where water lingers.
- On the other hand, *Fritillaria imperialis* and *F.elwesii* thrive in well-drained, drier conditions.

MAKING THE MOST OF WET AND DRY SPOTS

Understanding how water is distributed across your garden allows you to make informed decisions about watering and irrigation:

Wet areas: Plant water-loving species in damp spots to minimize the need for supplementary watering. **Wet loving examples:** Astilbe, meadowsweet (*filipendula ulmaria*), yellow flag iris, hosta, *Persicaria bistorta, Primula*

Dry areas: Opt for drought-tolerant plants in naturally dry locations to reduce water usage and create a low-maintenance garden. Check the plant map for more information. **Drought tolerant plants:** Lavender, sedum (*hylotelphium*), *Eryngium*, stachys, *Achillea millefolium*

There is further information on creating ponds and water features in your garden on pages 138–41, and advice on watering and irrigation in the garden on pages 198–9.

LIGHT

Making the most of light and shade

Once you start noticing how the light moves through your garden and mapping it out, which corners catch the first sun, where the shadows fall, how things shift as the day stretches on, you begin to understand your space in a whole new way. It's like learning its natural rhythm. Placing plants where they'll be happiest means they'll thrive more easily, reaching for the light or nestling into the shade just as they need.

When you work with the light, rather than against it, the garden responds. It grows with more ease, more beauty, more life. Some spots will glow with colour and warmth, others will hum with shady green calm. Tuning into this dance of light and shade can help you shape a space that not only looks good, but feels deeply alive and will help you unlock the full potential of your space.

Yew topiary balls, *Narcissus* 'Tête-à-tête', and *Euphorbia wulfenii* in early spring in the perennial border

HOW LIGHT INFLUENCES DESIGN

Light feeds different plants in different ways, according to their needs, and this, of course will affect what plants you choose for shady and sunny spots. But beyond that, it is light that can transform the entire atmosphere of your outdoor space at different times of day. There are no times more magical than at dawn, or dusk, golden hours when soft syrupy light casts a glow over your space. It's when birds sing their loudest, and plants with delicate architecture seem to light up with an almost ethereal beauty.

Light also shapes how your experience your garden in your day to day life, it will help you to strategically zone (see page 43) placing seating areas in spots that chase the sun, or dining spots that make the most of the shade. Your whole layout and planting plant will be mapped out by the way the light falls in your space!

LIGHT AND SHADE IN YOUR GARDEN

Understanding how light moves through your garden is essential for making the most of it. In fact, I think it is the most influential factor because it dictates what you can plant and where, how your plants will grow and, in turn, how you will use the space yourself.

Start by observing:

- *Where does the sun rise and set?*
- *What obstructions (trees, walls, buildings) impact the sun's journey?*
- *Where does the shade fall, and for how long at different times of the day?*

SHADE AS A FEATURE

Full shade is a concern that has come up again and again in people's questions about gardening. A shady garden doesn't have to be a challenge, but instead an opportunity. There are still lots of beautiful plant choices for shade and with thoughtfully placed plants and use of structures can maximize the natural cooling effects of shade during hot summer months. If you imagine working or dining in your garden in the summertime, then consider planning your plot around a shady, sheltered spot, surrounded by lush greenery that creates a calm, inviting retreat.

PLANTS AND LIGHT

Different plants thrive in different light conditions, and understanding how light interacts with your garden helps you choose the right ones for each spot. Some, such as sunflowers, bask happily in full sun, while others, such as hellebores and hostas, prefer the cool embrace of shade.

Interestingly, some plants even change colour depending on the intensity of light they receive. A few sweet pea varieties, like 'Henry Eckford' for example, can fade or 'burn' in intense sunlight, so when I grow them for floristry work, I ensure they are planted in a spot that has partial shade, avoiding the harshest sun to preserve their purest hues.

UNDERSTANDING SUNLIGHT REQUIREMENTS

Full sun: Plants that thrive in full sun need at least 6 hours of direct sunlight daily during midsummer. These are ideal for open, sunny spaces. **Examples:** cosmos, coneflowers, rosemary.

Partial shade: Requiring 3–6 hours of sunlight per day, these plants do well in areas with some shelter from the intense midday sun. **Examples:** hostas, astrantia, bleeding hearts.

Full shade: Best suited for spaces with less than 2–3 hours of direct sunlight per day, such as under tree canopies or along shaded walls. **Examples**: lungwort, brunnera.

Deep shade: Plants need minimal light, less than 2 hours of sunlight daily. These conditions are common under dense tree cover or heavy overhangs. **Examples:** bugleweed, sweet woodruf.

GARDEN DESIGN

APPROACHING THE PLAN

Planning with purpose and potential

All gardens have their limitations, but getting to grips with them and embracing them can help unlock the boundless creativity that is a bedfellow of restrictions. The ultimate advice for a happy, healthy and, above all, sustainable garden is to let your site lead and guide you on the design choices.

While all the choices you make are best determined by the conditions, it's still vital to prioritize your needs. The design of your garden has to maximize your eventual use of it. It's the very first thing to think about – how you want to use the space and how much time you have to give it in maintenance. After that there are many other tools and concepts you can work with, such as style and species variety, and I will walk you through them all.

A NOTE ON STYLE

The loveliest gardens to be in, I think, are an extension of those who tend to them. In this section I will guide you through my style in plants and materials and how I've grown my garden with them. There is no right or wrong style – remember that your style is the best style for your plot, so choose to surround yourself with plants and colours that light you up, and ones that your garden conditions will love too.

INTEGRATING BIODIVERSITY INTO YOUR DESIGN

A place where flowers sway, butterflies land on your shoulder and birds serenade you, these are the things that make a garden irresistible for me. Every one of us will have a different idea of a dream garden; mine is a place that is both productive and beautiful, and always teeming with life. Flat lawns and meticulous borders can diminish the space for wildlife, insects and biodiversity, and by designing and paring back in this way, you run the risk of creating a space that doesn't attract life. For the most biodiverse garden, we want to attract bugs, birds and bees, as well as giving them habitat to return to year after year.

Biodiversity, as I interpret it, is the quiet brilliance at the heart of the natural world, a vast and delicate web of life, where every plant, creature and habitat has a role, a rhythm, a relationship. It's not just the number of species, but how they live together: how a bee finds its flower, how a berry feeds a bird, how fungi knit through the forest floor like unseen threads holding everything together. It's life at its most alive, full of complexity, beauty and balance. And it's this interconnectedness that brings strength and softness to the world around us.

The term biodiversity originates from the Greek word *bios* (*βίος*), meaning 'life', and the Latin word *diversitas*, meaning 'variety' or 'difference'. Together, biodiversity literally translates to the 'variety of life'. Quite simply, it means the richness of life in all its forms, from the smallest microorganism to the tallest tree, and every relationship in between. I think gardens should honour that, not just as places of beauty, but as small, places of belonging and care, where life in all its diversity can root, stretch and thrive.

A GARDEN FOR INSPIRATION: KNEPP REWILDED GARDEN

A lot of what I have learned about encouraging biodiversity, and how to create a space which is harmonious for all types of nature, has come from one of my all-time favourite gardeners, Charlie Harpur. Charlie is currently the head gardener at The Knepp Rewilding Project in Sussex, a project that showcases the incredible potential of gardens to support biodiversity and reimagine how our gardens can function as dynamic ecosystems. Charlie's work centres on trialling potential conditions of the future and recording how different plant species react. Within Knepp's walled garden, the focus shifts from the castle's traditional manicured lawns to creating a complex mosaic of habitats teeming with life. Guided by experts like Tom Stuart-Smith and James Hitchmough, the project demonstrates how thoughtful interventions, such as introducing varied soil conditions, embracing undulating topography and selecting a wide range of plants, can spark ecological variety and complexity.

In the Rewilded Garden, over 900 species were planted to establish resilient plant communities, with the garden's evolution guided by nature itself. Gravel paths now bloom with herbs, and a former croquet lawn has been transformed into diverse hummocks that encourage native plants to seed. As 'rewilding gardeners', Charlie and his team at Knepp encourage minimal intervention, focusing on fostering greater complexity while accepting natural winners and losers, proving that even on a smaller scale, our own gardens can play a critical role in reversing biodiversity loss.

REASONS TO EMBRACE BIODIVERSITY IN YOUR PLANTING PLANS

Embracing a wide variety of plants in your garden isn't just good for the environment; it makes your space more beautiful, resilient and alive. Here are some of my favourite reasons to make biodiversity a priority.

Soil health improvement: Different plant roots work together to improve soil structure and health. A biodiverse garden enhances nutrient cycling, boosts beneficial soil microbes and even helps prevent erosion.

Rich wildlife habitat: A diverse garden comes from planting a rich variety of plant species, which in turn creates shelter and habitat for birds, small mammals, beneficial insects and pollinators. The more life your garden supports, the more vibrant and alive it becomes. There's nothing like seeing your garden teeming with wildlife to make you feel connected to the natural world and life itself. It becomes a space that is much more likely to be a balanced, self-sustaining ecosystem where everything can work together in harmony.

Pest control: Biodiversity helps keep less welcome creatures in check naturally. Some plants repel less welcome creatures, while others attract beneficial predators such as ladybirds and lacewings, that will help control unwanted visitors. It's nature's way of balancing the scales.

Increased resilience: Biodiverse gardens are naturally more resilient to less welcome creatures, diseases and even extreme weather. With a mix of species, your garden is better equipped to adapt to environmental changes and bounce back from challenges.

Pollinator support: Planting a variety of blooms provides food and habitat for essential pollinators such as bees and butterflies. These creatures are vital for food production and the overall health of our environment. Watching them flit and buzz through your garden is a joy in itself. We've kept bees for almost a decade now, and I love having them at the forefront of my mind when choosing plants to grow even in the leaner winter and early spring months.

Aesthetic appeal: It's beautiful: Having a garden filled with biodiversity can be a feast for the senses. It will be a space alive with humming bees, swooping birds, and croaking frogs. Walking through the garden in summer, butterflies dance around me as I walk, and these are the moments in life that I feel most connected to and uplifted by the world around me. A garden that is beautiful and vibrant, with a variety of plans offering different colours, textures and forms across the seasons, will always have something stunning to offer you.

WAYS TO ENCOURAGE BIODIVERSITY IN YOUR GARDEN

START WITH TOPOGRAPHY

On a late summer walk last year with Charlie Harpur (see page 34), I asked him what pointers he would give as easy ways to create garden spaces that are brimming with life. He suggested that one of the simplest ways to support biodiversity is to embrace the difference in topography in your soil, no matter how slight that may be.

Feel free to add a flat area for seating or for games, but if you are aiming for a healthy, sustainable and wildlife-friendly garden, avoid flattening your entire plot purely for the sake of aesthetics. Let your garden's natural contours shine, and work with them to support both beauty and biodiversity. Water moves in different ways according to how the earth lies, and by creating a mosaic pattern in your space, with each part consisting of minute and complex differences, such as changes in topography, the more extensive the range of creatures that can exist there. This is the making of biodiversity and, ultimately, a healthier, more sustainable and life-giving garden.

BALANCING CONTROL AND WILDNESS

A garden full of life requires a balance between intentional design and allowing nature to take its course. When it comes to editing and curating unwanted visitors in the form of pests and weeds, it's worth remembering that the more life you offer, the more life you will encounter, and with more complex diversity, the more resilient your space will be. And, although there's an argument in there somewhere for welcoming all plants, I still have a pretty low tolerance for bindweed (see how to weed on page 216). Even though bindweed provides food for the convolvulus hawkmoth and the elephant hawk-moth, both found here in my patch in Sussex, I still do as much as I can to remove it by hand each season as it can strangle and overwhelm the plants it grows among.

Bluebells and wild garlic

UNEDITED SPACES

Leaving a few corners of your garden untouched allows the uninvited plants you might not particularly love (bindweed, I'm still looking at you) to thrive and support life within your garden, regardless of your personal feelings about them. If you're concerned about unwanted plants taking over, rest assured – they don't have to remain completely unmanaged. There is a delicate balance to be maintained between manicured and wild spaces, fostering a harmonious coexistence.

Allowing some plants to live freely in your garden can significantly benefit the wider ecosystem. These plants provide habitat and food for various creatures, enhancing biodiversity and promoting a healthy garden environment. To manage this cohabitation effectively, follow these steps:

Research unedited plants: Identify the plants that naturally appear in your unmanaged areas. Understanding their growth habits, benefits and potential drawbacks is crucial.

Understand their role: Learn which creatures rely on these plants. Whether it's pollinators, such as bees and butterflies, or beneficial insects and birds, knowing their role can help you appreciate the value they bring to your garden.

Make informed decisions: With this knowledge, you can decide whether to keep these plants or manage them more actively. If a plant supports important wildlife and doesn't over-dominate the space, it might be worth allowing it to stay. Conversely, if it becomes invasive or detracts from your garden's overall design, targeted management can keep it in check.

Maintain balance: Strive for an endless balance between manicured and wild areas. This balance ensures that your garden remains both beautiful and ecologically supportive. Regular monitoring as well as the occasional adjustments will help maintain this equilibrium.

MANAGING INVASIVE PLANTS

For plants with invasive tendencies, proactive management helps to prevent them from overtaking your garden while still reaping their benefits for wildlife. Take buddleia, for example. I love it for attracting butterflies, but its invasive nature requires careful handling. In my garden, we always stop buddleia from setting seed, though a few have managed to establish themselves independently. During the summer, these plants become a haven for peacock, red admiral, small tortoiseshell and painted lady butterflies, filling the air with a delightful honey scent.

To maintain balance, I cut back buddleia as soon as the flowers start to fade and before the seeds will set. This practice ensures that the plant continues to provide a sanctuary for beautiful butterflies without dominating the garden or encroaching on the wild areas beyond its borders. With regular trimming, buddleia remains a valuable asset to the ecosystem without becoming a nuisance.

However, if a plant is highly invasive and poses a threat to native species, the best practice is to remove it entirely and dispose of it responsibly. Destroy, bury, or burn plant material on site whenever you can. Keep in mind that home compost systems might not get hot enough to completely eliminate all roots, stems and seeds. The UK's Department for Environment, Food and Rural Affairs (DEFRA) recommends that this material can also be processed as standard green waste through your local recycling programme.

A SIMPLE BUG HOTEL

Bug hotels are simple shelters that boost garden biodiversity by giving insects and other wildlife a safe haven. They support beneficial creatures that help control pests and pollinate plants. You can make a bug hotel as basic as a pile of sticks, twigs and leaves tucked away in a quiet corner.

Decaying wood is especially valuable for wildlife. To create a log-pile bug hotel, collect small logs, large sticks and pieces of rotting wood. Pile them up in a damp, shady spot in your garden, then stuff dead leaves into the nooks and crannies to make it cosy. This natural retreat is perfect for centipedes, woodlice and beetles, which love burrowing into decaying wood, and it might even attract birds, frogs and hedgehogs looking for a tasty snack.

THE REALITY OF TIME IN THE GARDEN

A garden is a living thing, and like anything alive, it needs time, love and attention. But the truth is, our lives change, and the time we can dedicate to our gardens fluctuates. In my case, I still gather plenty of ingredients for floristry work, harvest seeds for the business, and enjoy the garden as a haven. But life has changed in the last ten years and the reality of balancing a toddler, a growing business and another plot has forced me to prioritize. Since my business partner, Paris, and I started renting an additional acre for our cut-flower and seed business a few miles down the road, my home garden has had to adapt. A plot that once received hours of daily attention now gets just 3–6 hours a week. While that's less than I'd love to give it for its size, it's still enough to keep the garden generous, beautiful and productive for my family's needs.

Over this last growing season, I began to look at ways to make my home garden more manageable. While you think a garden might be something to expand and expand, the field I farm, and my toddler needed to take priority. I began by cutting back on the high-maintenance spaces, like a few of the annual growing beds. While I love their abundance, they're the most demanding part of the garden. Some have been transformed, simply by seeding, back to grass for my son to run on. Another part, I have filled with robust, low-maintenance perennials that I took from cuttings, providing a space that still offers beauty and ingredients, but requires far less attention.

Gardens evolve with our lives. Whether you're just starting out or scaling back, there's always a way to adjust your garden to fit the time, energy and love you have to give. With thoughtful planning and an openness to change, your garden can remain a source of joy no matter how much – or how little – time you can dedicate to it. As soon as the garden feels like a chore, or it becomes overwhelming, it's a sign to adapt it to fit your life and design it to be more manageable.

One of my favourite parts of the garden is our small orchard of eight fruit trees. It perfectly balances beauty and low maintenance. This area performs as a a garden that doesn't have to demand constant effort to be magical. We mow the orchard just once a year, leaving winding paths through the meadow grasses that we trim every few weeks. These simple paths are a delight to walk, and give the space a natural, flowing feel.

Bulbs planted in the grass provide a stunning display for months. In late winter, snowdrops and crocuses emerge, followed by *Leucojums*, narcissi and camassias in spring. By midsummer, martagon lilies add height and elegance. Rugged roses, fruiting branches, and teasels extend the season into autumn, with spindle berries adding vibrant splashes of colour. Even in winter, the lichen covered branches of the fruit trees stand like sculptures, offering a bare beauty that I love.

The orchard is a space that feels full of life yet requires very little from me in return. It provides cuttings for the house, interest for wildlife and a seasonal flow of beauty that changes effortlessly through the year. Even when time is limited, perhaps just planting one fruit tree and allowing a small surrounding area around it to be low maintenance but filled with wildflowers and different bulbs that bloom across the seasons, you can create a garden that works for you, a space that supports your life rather than demanding all of it.

Narcissus 'Tahiti', 'Skype' and 'Mother Duck' under a cherry tree

MANAGING EXPECTATIONS AND GARDEN TIME

When creating a garden, it's easy to focus on the planning and planting stages while overlooking the ongoing commitment a garden requires. A garden isn't just a one-time project; it's a continuous relationship that evolves over the years. Being realistic about how much time you have, and how much time you *want* to spend, will shape your garden's layout, design and plant choices.

The best gardens aren't necessarily the ones tended to daily, although of course they are likely to be lovely and loved; a thoughtfully planned garden with self-sufficient planting can still be beautiful, productive and seasonally interesting, even with minimal maintenance. **Ask yourself, how much time do you have or, more importantly, *want* to spend on it?**

Phacelia tanacetifolia and *Alchemilla mollis* in the peony beds

HOW TO PLAN YOUR GARDEN BASED ON YOUR AVAILABLE TIME

The size of your garden will also alter the amount of time needed to tend to it. The UK average is about 200 square metres (2,152 square feet). These projections of time spent gardening are with those sized gardens in mind, up to half an acre.

1–4 times a year: Opt for low-maintenance plants and landscaping, such as a meadow or small orchard. Choose hardy plants that thrive with little intervention.

1–4 hours a month: A primarily low-maintenance garden with perennials and a few annuals is achievable. Select plants that require minimal weeding or care, and focus on easy-to-manage borders or containers. Choosing a few plants that can establish a good ground cover, such as creeping thyme, low-growing sedum or clover, will help with weed management, and limit evaporation from the soil in hot weather. It would still be wise to have a simple irrigation system to help your plants manage through hot weather.

1–4 hours a week: You'll have enough time to enjoy a relaxed potter in the garden, care for annuals, maintain a small lawn and tend to containers and borders. It would be wise to install a simple irrigation system to water when you don't have time.

1–4+ hours a day: With time to dedicate daily, the possibilities are endless. You can plant whatever you like, create diverse spaces and maintain larger areas, tailoring the landscape to your vision.

HOW TO DESIGN A GARDEN THAT WORKS FOR YOU

Your garden is an extension of your home, and how you envision using it will shape its flow and design. Whether it's a place to relax, entertain, grow food or connect with nature, defining your priorities will help guide your choices. A well-thought-out garden can meet multiple needs, providing areas for tranquillity, productivity and play. How do you want to use your garden?

Here are some ideas to help you tailor your garden to suit you and the life you want to live in it.

Eat in it: Prioritize a comfortable spot to sit, whether in the sun or shade, depending on your preference. Think about the times you're most likely to use it – would you enjoy breakfast or dinner outdoors? Or, if you work from home, do you need a lunchtime retreat away from your desk?

Entertain in it: Designate an area where guests can sit or stand comfortably. Create a welcoming space for gatherings, with room for a table, chairs and perhaps some soft lighting for evening entertainment.

Play in it: If you like using your outdoor space for sprawling games of cards or for playing sport, you'll want to make some areas for that. Likewise, if you have pets or children, it might be your priority to include a lawn for games, a shaded corner for quiet play, or areas for exploration. For pets, consider some pet-friendly planting, which basically means avoiding toxic favourites, such as lilies, foxgloves and daffodils.

Potter in it: For those who love to tinker and tend, centre your design around large borders that require care and attention. Include plenty of planting areas, along with well-organized storage for tools.

Reflect in it: Create a tranquil space with sensory elements such as fragrant plants, soft textures and the soothing sound of water. A solitary seat tucked into a quiet corner can provide the perfect retreat for reflection.

Commune with nature in it: Focus on planting wildlife-friendly species and creating habitats that invite birds, bees, butterflies and other creatures. A wildlife pond or bug hotel (see page 37) can enhance the connection to nature.

Grow ingredients in it: Dedicate part of your garden to growing vegetables, fruit, or flowers for cutting. If you're not direct sowing, consider adding a potting area and cold frames. You might have a greenhouse in mind as a place to start seedlings (this can be of any size, from a miniature one against a wall, all the way up to a grander scale depending on your space and needs). You might want a place to store tools, too.

Narcissus 'White Marvel' and 'Bellsong', Tulip 'La Belle Epoque', Wallflower 'Sunset Apricot', and *Fritillaria imperialis* 'Orange Beauty' in the Well Garden in spring

ALLOCATING A SPACE

Making room for what matters

Now that we've gone through your gardens unique quirks, its light, soil, rhythms, and we've thought about your needs and goals with the space, you can begin to shape your garden into a place that feels both purposeful and personal.

In the garden design world, the next step is called 'zoning'. Creating 'zones' within the space is simply about imagining how you'd like to divide it up, no matter the size, and live in each part.

Whether it's a shady corner to sit with a cup of tea, a patch for growing herbs by the kitchen, or a bed that bursts with colour through the year, zoning allows you to organize your space around the ways you want to move, rest and grow within it.

No matter the size of your garden, this next step helps turn it into somewhere that's beautiful and nurturing, a place that works with your life, season by season. In this next section I'll talk you through some simple ways to approach and think about zoning.

Pelargoniums on the table with floral arrangements with calendulas and *Nasturtiums. Heuchera* 'Marmalade' and *Pittosporum* 'Pompom' in pots.

EVALUATE YOUR SPACE

Take a close look at your garden's size, shape and features.

Sun and shade: Where does the sunlight fall, and for how long? Use sunny spots for activities, such as growing vegetables or eating meals.

Existing structures: Note trees, slopes and fences that can act as anchors for your design.

Viewlines: What do you see from different areas? Mask unsightly views, highlight beautiful ones and celebrate borrowed scenery (such as a neighbour's tree).

Practicalities: Consider drainage, privacy, access points, soil type, water source points (such as taps and water butts), and the overall climate to inform what works best where.

CREATE ZONES

Breaking your garden into zones adds clarity and flow. These zones help prioritize activities and simplify maintenance. For example:

Entertainment zone: A patio with a table and chairs for dining and gatherings.

Productive zone: Cultivation beds in a sunny spot for vegetables, fruit, herbs or flowers.

Relaxation zone: A shaded seating area for reading or meditating.

MAPPING YOUR GARDEN

Mapping your garden visually is a simple way to make your ideas tangible.

You will need

- Pen
- Paper
- Tracing paper
- A printed aerial view of your garden (optional; may be available from online maps)

Step by step

1. *Sketch your base map*
   On a piece of paper draw your garden's boundaries, key features and existing plants you want to keep.

2. *Add layers*
   On a separate sheet of tracing paper, which can overlay the paper plan, note:

   Sunlight and shade: Identify areas of full sun, partial shade and deep shade.

   Proposed zones: Sketch potential locations for activities and adjust until it feels balanced.

   Design pathways: Connect zones with potential paths (see pages 46–7). These pathways guide movement and create a sense of exploration.

3. *Be open to change*
   The best garden designs are flexible. As your needs evolve or plants grow, your zones may need adjustment. A few years ago, I transformed a long, unused grass corridor into a cut-flower garden. By shifting shrubs, removing a fence and adding beds and pathways, this area became the heart of my garden. The bottom line is: don't be afraid to experiment and let your garden guide you.

MY GARDEN
& ITS ZONES
1
2
3
4
5
6
10
11
13
14
15
16
17
18
19
N
W
E
S

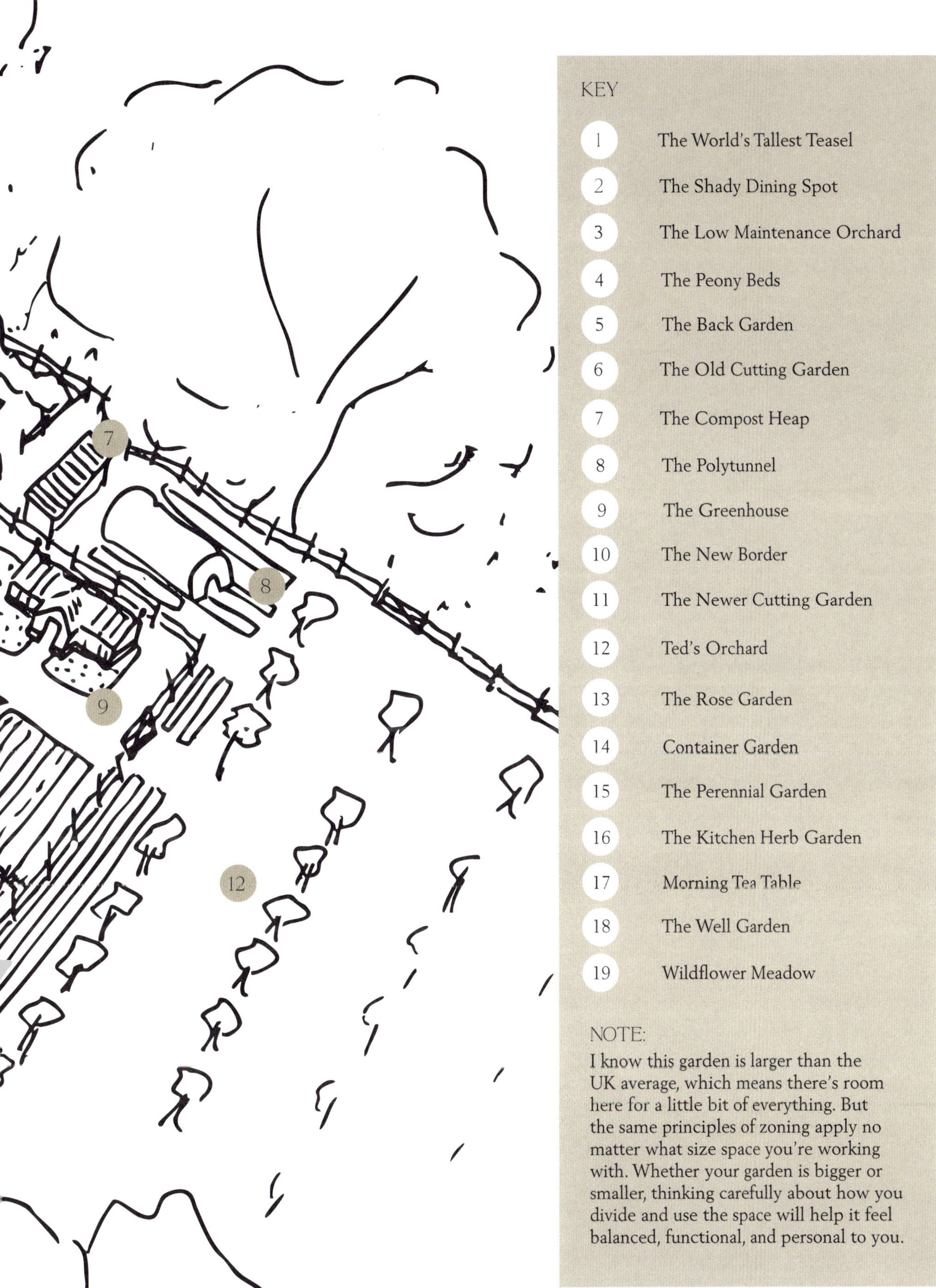

NOTE:
I know this garden is larger than the UK average, which means there's room here for a little bit of everything. But the same principles of zoning apply no matter what size space you're working with. Whether your garden is bigger or smaller, thinking carefully about how you divide and use the space will help it feel balanced, functional, and personal to you.

PATHS & BOUNDARIES

Creating structure and guiding flow

Once you've mapped out the different areas and functional zones of your garden, take a walk through it. Notice how it feels to move from one space to another. Does the layout flow? Is there ease in how you move, and do the paths invite you in?

This is the moment to think about where to shape paths and intuitive boundaries, the lines that guide your steps and frame the beauty. For walkways meant to be shared or slowly wandered, a width of around 1.2 metre (4 feet) allows two people to walk side by side, or gives space for a wheelchair to move through comfortably. These small considerations help make the garden feel generous and welcoming.

Rose 'Cécile Brunner'

PATHS

Design paths that naturally guide movement through your garden. They should connect zones seamlessly, making it easy to travel between them. Think about how you'll use these paths, do you want a quick, direct route from your kitchen door to your dining area, or a winding, meandering path to a tranquil seating spot?

Clare Foster, a writer and gardener I admire, shared the idea of allowing dogs to dictate pathway placement in a garden she visited. Their natural running patterns helped determine intuitive and practical routes, preventing damage to planted borders. I loved the idea of this playful and practical way to ensure this garden worked for everyone, including their pets.

PATH DESIGN IDEAS

Curved: Create a sense of mystery and exploration by designing gently curving paths that lead to hidden garden features.

Patterned paths: Incorporate geometric patterns, such as herringbone or circular designs, to add sophistication and interest to paved areas.

Integrated lighting: Install solar-powered or low-voltage lighting along paths to illuminate the way and highlight garden elements at night. *Note:* be aware of using lights if you are in live in an International Dark Sky Place (IDSP).

Complementary planting: Line paths with flowers, shrubs or ground cover to add colour and texture, creating a cohesive garden design. Creeping thyme or chamomile grown between pavers look attractive and release a lovely scent when stepped on.

Varying heights: Use steps, terraces or raised sections to navigate changes in elevation and add dimension.

Focal points: Direct the flow of paths towards focal points such as sculptures, fountains or seating areas to guide visitors' attention.

BOUNDARIES

Use boundaries like hedges, fencing or planting to separate zones and create a sense of intrigue. A well-placed gate or archway can add an element of surprise, encouraging curiosity and exploration. Playful touches like these make your garden feel inviting and dynamic. Hedges and boundaries can simply offer a sense of place, too, by acting as the bones of your space.

PLANTS FOR HEDGES

These are some of my favourite plants to use as hedging:

Beech (kept cropped), berberis, climbing roses, crab apple, guelder rose, hawthorn, hazel, holly, honeysuckle (especially the shrubby honeysuckle *Lonicera nitida*), hornbeam, privet, spindle berry, *Viburnum tinus*.

Fruiting hedge: apple, blackberry, damson, pear, plum, sloe (low-growing stepover fruit trees can make especially lovely short boundary fences).

MATERIALS

Choosing the right elements for form and function

Every garden begins with a dialogue between the living and the lasting; plants that change with the seasons, and the materials that hold them in place. The stones beneath your feet, the path that leads you through the planting, the handmade gate that swings open to welcome you in, these elements shape how we move through a garden, how we rest in it, and how it endures through time.

While plants bring movement, scent and life, materials offer structure, rhythm and a kind of permanence. The best gardens, I think, strike a gentle balance between the two, allowing each to elevate the other. It's worth choosing materials with intention, as they are the things that will likely last long after we move on.

HARDSCAPING V SOFTSCAPING

Hardscaping refers to the non-living structural elements in a garden, such as patios, pathways and walls, while softscaping focuses on the living, dynamic parts of the garden, such as plants, trees and lawns. Striking a balance between the two is key to creating a garden that is both functional and attractive.

Although I will discuss how to approach the hardscaping elements to your garden in this section, this is not a book on either hardscaping design or DIY hardscaping. My approach to gardening is about creating a garden that won't go out of style whilst spending less money and fewer resources in the process. I would always opt for softscaping techniques, preferring plants to concrete landscaping. I prefer how it looks, that it provides additional habitat and that it costs much less.

While there are occasions when a patio or solid path might be the most appropriate choice to allow you to use parts of your garden how you would like, I hope to encourage you away from using loads of hardscaping elements and towards what a garden should really be all about, the plants and the life that they support.

CHOOSING MATERIALS

The materials you choose for your garden are just as important as the plants you grow. The paths, fences, and walls form the bare bones of your space, providing structure and helping your garden to look beautiful in every season.

On the flipside, softscaping can still be just as good at providing framework. Softscaping with evergreens can provide the winter structure beautifully, and even many herbaceous perennials are beautiful well past their prime in their seed-head form, left to stand all winter. A garden chosen for statuesque seedheads, even without shrubs and hardscaping, can still be exquisite all year round. I am especially fond of *Phlomis* for this purpose, and I leave the architectural stems standing until spring.

TIPS FOR CHOOSING MATERIALS

Choosing materials is a balance of practicality and creating a garden that feels harmonious, no matter the season. The right choices will provide structure, beauty and a sense of permanence, letting your plants shine in their own time.

Limit your palette: This is not a hard and fast rule, but trying to stick to no more than three types of materials is an effective trick, as it help to keep your garden's structure simple, cohesive and visually pleasing, even if your planting is wild and chaotic.

Work with what you have: If you can't change existing features, such as fences or walls, use evergreen climbers or shrubs to soften or mask them.

Order samples: Before finalizing your selections, order samples to see how the materials work together. Feel them in your hands and get them wet to see how their colours change, this will help you to appreciate their true colours and textures in your garden's natural light.

Think about practicality: Hardscaping paths in well-trodden or high-traffic areas can make your garden easier to navigate and maintain year-round. Materials such as brick, paving, gravel or stone are durable options that help define zones, create flow and withstand heavy use. Brick, paved or cobbled paths, though more expensive than grass, dirt or woodchips, offer timeless charm and long-lasting durability, making them ideal for frequently used routes.

For less-travelled areas, wood-chip paths are a natural, cost-effective choice that's easy to replenish. While hard landscaping materials involve a higher upfront cost, they provide practical, low-maintenance solutions for ensuring year-round access, even in muddy conditions. Remember that most paths, whether soft or hard, require some level of upkeep, from mowing and edging grass paths to weeding or refreshing woodchips, and keeping hard surfaces, such as brick and stone, clear of slippery algae.

USING LOCAL MATERIALS

Your surroundings can inspire your material choices. My garden is enclosed by woods that include hazel around the edges and glades of coppiced chestnut further in. The materials we use for boundaries and plant support reflect this, so all my wobbly little fences are made from hazel and chestnut. The cottage has internally exposed brickwork throughout, so I replicated that by adding winding brick paths leading from the driveway to the back door and from the back door, to the studio. Elsewhere, I've kept it simple, with mown grass paths that echo the meadows beyond.

Look at what's around you – if your garden is near brick buildings, brick paths or walls might feel natural. If you're by the coast, shingle or driftwood could be ideal. Choosing materials that reflect your environment helps your garden feel connected to its surroundings.

Ultimately, your choice of materials should align with your garden's style, your budget and how you plan to use the space. Here are some options to consider (see also page 136 for information on installing a path).

NATURAL STONE PAVERS

Slate, granite or flagstone pavers: Durable and provide excellent traction but also offer a natural and elegant appearance. Perfect for creating intricate designs and patterns.

Pros: Long-lasting, aesthetically pleasing and available in various colours and textures. Flexible design options, durable and easy to replace individual pieces.

Cons: Can be expensive, need a stable base and may require professional installation.

GRAVEL AND CRUSHED STONE

Pea gravel, river rock or crushed granite: Ideal for informal or rustic gardens.

Pros: Affordable, easy to install and allow good drainage.

Cons: Can shift over time, require replenishing and may need regular weeding to prevent unwanted plants from taking hold.

BRICK

Clay bricks: Classic choice that adds warmth and colour to paths.

Pros: Durable, easy to lay in patterns and provides a timeless look.

Cons: Can be slippery when wet and may require maintenance to prevent weed growth.

CONCRETE

Stamped or stained concrete: Versatile and can mimic other materials, such as stone or brick.

Pros: Highly durable, low maintenance and customizable in terms of colour and texture.

Cons: Can crack over time, requires sealing and is not environmentally friendly due to high energy consumption and carbon footprint during production.

MULCH AND WOOD CHIPS

Organic mulches: Suitable for naturalistic or woodland gardens.

Pros: Soft walking surface, affordable and easy to install.

Cons: Requires regular replenishing and can be messy.

COBBLES

Cobbles or setts: Naturally occurring rounded stones, or quarried and shaped stones. Often reclaimed and give a richly textured and traditional surface that feels firmly rooted in place and history.

Pros: Beautifully characterful, extremely durable. Very low maintenance once laid.

Cons: Can be uneven to walk on, making them less suitable for accessibility. Installation can be labour intensive.

Tulip *'Purissima'* along the brick path in spring

HOW TO CHOOSE THE PLANTING

There are a few questions that can help ease the overwhelm of choosing what to plant, but I think this might be the most important of all: how do you want the garden to feel? It's something I often ask clients when selecting flowers for a wedding or event, because atmosphere goes far beyond colour palettes or trends. It's the emotional centre of a space, the thing that lingers.

Plants have a remarkable ability to carry mood. Just like the way we fill our homes with layers of texture and colour to reflect who we are, we can shape the garden with planting, layout, materials and even furniture to express feeling, and bring a garden to life with its own identity.

When I began the garden here, I knew I wanted it to feel rooted in the wider landscape but also full of joy, softness, texture and abundance. Back then, I was commuting to the city and often only saw the garden in the half-light. So I chose pale plants in soft pinks and creams, that bloomed in autumn, winter and early spring, the darker ends of the year, because they seemed to glow in low light, catching the moon or the last threads of dusk. It meant that even on the greyest days, I came home to something that lifted me. The best kind of small joys.

Hydrangea 'Limelight', *Pittorporum* 'Golf Ball', *Geranium* 'Rozanne', *Erigeron*, *Lavandula angustifolia* 'Hidcote'

Alpine strawberries, *Alchemilla mollis*, *Erigeron*, *Polystichum polyblepharum* (Japanese lace fern)

IDEAS FOR TRANSLATING MOOD INTO PLANTING

Here are some suggestions to help you reflect mood and atmosphere in your planting choices:

Calm: Focus on a muted colour palette and ensure there's a comfortable, obvious place to sit.

Uplifting: Choose plants with scents you love and colours that bring you happiness.

Joyful: Use a brighter colour palette and aim for seasonal, ever-changing interest to spark joy year-round.

Sensual: Incorporate plants with a variety of textures, such as grasses and evergreens, and include strongly scented plants.

Sleek: Opt for a pared-back design with formal layouts, straight lines and fewer plants.

Casual: Pick plants with informal structures and include soft curves in borders, paths and grass edges.

Relaxing: Use swaying perennials and ornamental grasses to soften the planting, and consider adding a water feature to create gentle movement.

INSPIRATION FOR YOUR GARDEN STYLE

Inspiration for your garden can come from countless places. It could be the way shrubs are arranged in a hedgerow, the mingling of wildflowers and grasses at the edge of a field, or combinations admired in other gardens. These moments of inspiration can often be easily translated into your own garden.

Visiting gardens is one of my favourite ways to collect inspiration. Each one has its own unique character, and while nothing compares to experiencing a garden in person, we're lucky to live in a time where virtual visits are possible. Online platforms offer endless imagery to explore, and books are a treasure trove. Garden design books filled with tumbling roses, swaying daisies or rows of vegetables can offer incredible starting points for your vision.

Inspiration can also come from unexpected sources, even inanimate objects. Walking through towns and cities, I often notice unintentional colour combinations, such as faded shop shutters alongside weathered windows, that spark new ideas. Growing up in London, I was fascinated by how some plants thrive in tough conditions, such as a tenacious *Campanula portenschlagiana* shooting up through pavement cracks or blooming in the most unlikely corners. These observations have influenced my choices for hardy plants that are perfect for tucking into walls or tricky spots in my own garden.

Art has also played a significant role in shaping my garden. The floral paintings of Rachel Ruysch, a renowned Dutch Golden Age artist, have inspired me for years as a floral designer. Her works led me to grow tulips such as *Estella Rijnveld*, a striking striped parrot variety reminiscent of the bold blooms she painted. It's a divisive choice for some, but every spring when these tulips reappear, they fill me with joy.

Above: Sweet peas 'Mollie Rilstone', 'Ballerina Blue', 'Aphrodite', and 'Alisa'

Right: Rose 'Olivia Rose Austin'

MAKING A VISION BOARD

I love making and using a vision board as I find it much easier to conceptualise and visualise tangible things rather than just seeing information on a screen. Creating one is a wonderful way to bring your inspirations together and start shaping a cohesive plan for your garden. It's an intuitive, creative process that works perfectly on a grey, miserable day when you want to dream about your outdoor space. By gathering photos, objects and mementos that weave ideas together, you can lay the groundwork for a thoughtful and actionable design.

WHAT TO INCLUDE IN YOUR VISION BOARD

- Photos from gardens you've visited.
- Flowers or foliage you've collected.
- Material samples, such as paving or fencing options.
- Fabric swatches or paint chips for outdoor walls or furniture.
- Plant images cut out from catalogues and magazines.

HOW TO USE A VISION BOARD

Arrange and rearrange: Move items around to see how they work together. Pair colours, materials and plant images to test combinations.

Edit and simplify: Remove anything that feels out of place. Limit the colours and materials to keep the design cohesive.

Explore options: Try different colours next to each other to find combinations that excite you. Consider materials for paths, fences or gates, and order samples if needed. Think about the furniture you'd like to include.

Plan for seasons: Group plant choices by season to ensure year-round interest (see pages 77–83 for more on interest through the season).

Refine your vision: Use the vision board to clarify the plants, materials and colours you're gravitating towards and start shaping your design.

• Snowdrops
• Leucojum
• Crocus
• Iris reticulata
Winter
Late Spring
• Tulip
• Fritillaria
• Aquilegia
• Dahlia
• Roses (repeat flowering types)
• Geranium
• Japanese Anemone

COLOUR IN THE GARDEN

Balance, contrast and clashes

Colour is deeply personal. When it comes to the garden, think of it as a canvas, ready to be explored and played with. Most rules about colour – yes, even the ones in this book – are there to guide, not dictate. The real priority is choosing plants that bring you joy. But there's an undeniable thrill in experimenting with how colours interact, inform and transform one another. For me, it's one of the most exhilarating parts of gardening: the sheer delight of experimenting with myriad colours.

The dominant colour in every garden is green. Unlike a painting, where colours can be uninterrupted and precise, a garden's colours are always impressionistic, ever-changing with the seasons and framed against a backdrop of leaves, stems and foliage. While there are plants with alternative foliage tones, green acts as a neutralizing force. It provides balance and helps prevent clashing, making it easier to combine bolder colours.

WHY CONSIDER A COLOUR PALETTE FOR YOUR GARDEN?

Choosing a colour palette for your garden isn't a suggestion to limit your creativity, it's about giving focus to your design. When you enter a plant nursery or garden centre, it's easy to fall in love with everything you see; as someone greedy for colour, I know this trap all too well. Having a palette in mind helps you stay intentional, choosing plants that complement one another and fit your garden's conditions.

That said, I don't believe in sticking rigidly to a single scheme. If you want a harmonious garden but don't know where to start, the tips in this section are for guidance. They're not hard rules – just tools to help you feel more confident about working with colour.

THE ROLE OF SEASONAL COLOUR

A garden isn't static; its colours shift and evolve throughout the year. In my garden, this transformation is best reflected in the permanent border around my home. It begins in spring with pale yellows and soft pinks, echoing the softness of a watercolour. As summer approaches, this intensifies into a bold and vibrant mosaic of colour and texture. By autumn, the border takes on the warmth and complexity of an oil painting, and by winter, it settles into a near-monochromatic palette of outlines and structures. This constant evolution makes the garden feel alive, offering something new and beautiful to enjoy in every season.

Peony 'Germaine Bigot', *Phacelia* and common foxglove

WORKING WITH COLOUR: A BEGINNER'S GUIDE

If you're new to gardening, the thought of choosing colours might feel overwhelming. Don't worry – you're not alone. Questions about colour are the ones I am asked the most! Here are some simple tips to help you get started.

Start simple: If too many colours feel chaotic, try reducing the number of different colours in one border. Simplifying can create a more cohesive look, especially in smaller spaces.

Stick to a colour family: If you're unsure, focus on one colour family. For example, shades of pinks, purples and lavenders can create a sense of flow without leading you into overthinking the design.

Let plants lead: Start with plants you already love. Build your palette around them, using complementary or contrasting tones (see page 64) to enhance their beauty.

Remember form and texture: Colour is fleeting – flowers fade, but shapes and textures endure. Give equal (if not more) importance to a plant's structure, foliage and form when planning your garden.

Take in your surroundings: Your garden doesn't exist in isolation – it is framed by its surroundings. If you have a dominating feature, such as a red brick wall or a yellow brick façade, see it as an opportunity to incorporate its tones into your palette. For instance, warm oranges, yellows and earthy reds can echo or complement red brick, while cool greens and soft whites can balance and soften it. By working with these existing elements, your garden can feel connected and cohesive.

Dahlia 'Cornel Bronze'

UNDERSTANDING THE COLOUR WHEEL

The colour wheel is a well-used tool for understanding how colours work together. Here's a quick refresher.

PRIMARY COLOURS

Red/yellow/blue

Primary colours are the building blocks of all other colours. They cannot be created by mixing other hues; they are pure and saturated. Their intensity gives them a strong presence, but this can also make them challenging to use effectively in garden design.

Primary colours provide vibrancy and impact and demand attention. Red is bold and passionate, yellow is cheerful and energizing, and blue is calming yet commanding. Because of their natural intensity, these colours to draw the eye immediately and can quickly dominate a space if overused.

Using primary colours in the garden

Red: Add drama with roses, salvias or poppies, but balance their boldness with plenty of neutral greens, softer pinks, or whites.

Yellow: Perfect for spring; acidic shades are great when paired with softer buttery hues, creams and fresh greens. Daffodils, tulips and narcissi can bring brightness without overwhelming.

Blue: Think delphiniums or cornflowers for a touch of cool elegance, especially in summer borders. I particularly enjoy layering blues with softer lavenders and mauves.

Design tip: When used together, primary colours can feel playful but may lean towards a childlike aesthetic. To create a more sophisticated look, use them sparingly as accent colours, or pair them with neutrals, softer tints, or muted tones see page 62.

SECONDARY COLOURS

Orange/green/purple

Secondary colours are created by mixing two primary colours. They are naturally more harmonious and versatile than pure primaries, offering a softer but still vibrant palette.

Using secondary colours in the garden

Orange: Bright and inherently warm, it pairs beautifully with cooler purples or blues for contrast. You can try dahlias, marigolds or *Cosmos sulphureus*.

Green: As the predominant colour in most gardens, green is often provided in a backdrop of trees, grass and foliage, against which other colours shine.

Purple: Can be dramatic or calming, purple can range from pale lavenders to rich, velvety violets.

Design tip: Secondary colours can act as bridges between primaries, softening the overall palette while adding richness and variety.

TERTIARY COLOURS

Blue-green/blue-violet/red-orange/red-violet/ yellow-orange/yellow-green

Tertiary colours are created by mixing a primary colour with a secondary colour. They offer endless possibilities for creating subtle colour schemes that feel both intricate and cohesive. Tertiary colours include shades such as turquoise (blue-green), magenta (red-violet) and chartreuse (yellow-green). They are less intense than primary or secondary colours, making them excellent for layering and softening bold palettes.

Using tertiary colours in the garden

Turquoise and chartreuse: Perfect for contemporary, playful designs.

Amber and vermilion: Add warmth and richness to autumnal borders.

Magenta and violet: Bring depth and drama to summer planting schemes.

Design tip: Tertiary colours are the most versatile for making bridges between colours. They can help pull colours together to make any design feel more harmonious.

HUE, TINT, TONE AND SHADE

Understanding the nuances of colour: hue, tint, tone and shade, can help you refine your planting choices and create a garden that feels intentional and balanced.

HUE

A hue is a pure colour, whether primary, secondary or tertiary, without any white, grey or black added. Think of it as the colour in its most vibrant form.

Design tip: Use pure hues as the foundation of your palette. They serve as bold focal points that can energize your garden design, especially when balanced with softer tints, refined tones or deeper shades.

TINTS

Tints (pictured below) are hues mixed with white, resulting in softer, pastel shades, such as baby pinks, pale blues or buttery yellows. These create a serene, cottage-style aesthetic.

Design tip: Tints have a tendency to be saccharine and associated with cottage gardens. If you are drawn to pastels, try adding a pure primary, secondary or tertiary colour to anchor, complement and unsweeten the scheme.

From left to right: Calendula 'Strawberry Blonde', Cosmos 'Cupcakes', *Nigella* 'Delft Blue', *Nasturtium* 'Tip Top Blush' and 'Tip Top Apricot', *Lavatera* 'Silver Blush', Rose 'Queen of Sweden', Sweet pea 'Ballerina Blue', *Nicotiana* 'Marshmallow', *Astilbe* 'Pretty in Pink, *Artemesia absinthium*, *Campanula* 'Pritchard's Variety' and 'Loddon Anna', Snapdragon 'Appleblossom'

TONES

Tones (pictured below) are created by mixing a hue with grey, which mutes the colour and creates a more sophisticated, subdued effect. We generally call these 'muted' colours as the vibrancy is taken out, leading to 'muddier' tones.

Toned-down colours, such as dusky pinks, muted lavenders and sage greens, work beautifully in both naturalistic and modern gardens.

Design tip: Use tones to create a cohesive, calming palette that doesn't overwhelm.

From left to right: Physocarpus 'Panther', *Dahlia* 'Burlesca', *Verbascum* 'Southern Charm', Rose 'Moka Rosa', *Pittosporum* 'Little Squirt', *Heuchera* 'Blackberry way' and 'Marmalade', *Sedum* 'Chocolate Cherry', *Nasturtium* 'Ladybird Rose', Rose 'Blue for You', *Pittosporum* 'Tom Thumb', Sweet pea 'Kings Ransom', Flowering oregano', *Euphorbia* 'Miners Merlot', *Setaria* 'Caramel', Poppy 'Pandora'

From left to right: Copper beech, *Dahlia* 'Moors Place', *Hibiscus acetosella* 'Mahogany Splendor', Orach 'Copper Plume', Cosmos 'Rubenza', *Scabiosa* 'Black Knight', Rose 'Darcey Bussell', *Melica altissima atropurpurea*, Sweet pea 'Windsor', *Malope* 'Vulcan', *Amaranth* 'Velvet Curtains', *Pittosporum* 'Tom Thumb', *Panicum violaceum*, Smokebush (*Cotinus*) 'Royal Purple'

SHADES

Shades (pictured above) are hues mixed with black, resulting in deeper, darker colours. Darker shades, such as burgundy, plum and midnight blue, add depth, drama and contrast.

Design tip: Shades can be used to create a sense of depth, richness and contrast, especially when combined with other colours.

BUILDING COLOUR PALETTES IN THE GARDEN

CONTRASTING COLOURS

Using contrasting colours in a garden creates an atmosphere that is dynamic, joyful and visually engaging. These colours, also known as complementary colours, sit opposite each other on the colour wheel: red and green, blue and orange, or yellow and purple. When paired, they amplify one another's vibrancy, creating a striking effect that draws the eye.

This phenomenon, known as simultaneous contrast, is rooted in how our eyes and brains process colour. Our photoreceptor cells, called cones, are sensitive to specific colour ranges: red, green and blue. When we focus on one colour for a while, the cone responsible becomes fatigued, making its complementary colour appear stronger by contrast. For example, after staring at a bright red flower, you might briefly see a green afterimage on a neutral background. This natural interplay enhances the intensity of complementary colours when placed side by side, making them feel even more vivid and alive.

From left to right: Nasturtium 'Whirlybird Cream', *Calendula* 'Snow Princess', Chive flower, *Lavatera clementii* 'Lilac Lady', *Phacelia*, Sweet pea 'David Tostevin', *Allium* 'Summer Beauty', Dill, Jasmine 'Clotted Cream', *Campanula* 'Loddon Anna', Rose 'Kew Gardens', Sweet pea 'Kippen Cream'

USING CONTRASTING COLOURS IN THE GARDEN

Red and green: Green is the backbone of most gardens, thanks to the abundance of foliage, making it an ideal base for contrasting with red. One of my favourite pairings uses the rose 'Darcey Bussell', as its velvety, crushed berry-red petals stand out beautifully against the glossy green foliage. I've planted these roses on either side of the steps outside my back door, underplanted with the thistle-like *Cirsium rivulare* 'Atropurpureum', a deep burgundy flower that enhances the drama.

Blue and orange: These two colours can be show-stopping when used together. There are some beautiful combinations, such as vibrant orange tagetes (marigolds) against a backdrop of cool blue cornflowers in the cutting garden, or brilliant orange tulips alongside the soft powder blue of forget-me-nots in spring.

Yellow and purple: These can be one of the trickiest contrasting combinations to execute, but when done right, it can be one of the most rewarding. I've experimented with this pairing in a gold-themed border, introducing the soft lavender tones of *Nepeta* and salvias alongside warm golden hues of *Nasturtiums* and roses. The result has been a joyful interplay of light and depth, transforming the space into something truly special. If you love bold contrasts but find them too intense, try using softer or more muted tones to achieve a gentler effect.

ANALOGOUS COLOURS

An analogous colour scheme uses colours that sit next to each other on the colour wheel, creating a naturally harmonious and calming effect. This approach helps your garden feel cohesive and peaceful, as these colours blend seamlessly.

CREATING AN ANALOGOUS COLOUR SCHEME

Choose a base colour: Start by selecting a colour that resonates with you. This could be a favourite hue or one that complements existing garden structures, such as walls, pathways or seating areas.

Identify neighbouring colours: On the colour wheel (page 68), identify two to four colours adjacent to your base colour. These hues will form your analogous palette. For example, if you choose green as your base, neighbouring colours might include blue-green and blue, creating a serene feel. Green, blue-green and blue form an easy, go-to colour palette. I often suggest a hardworking plant list in blues to friends who are just starting out with a border. The list nearly always features *Geranium* 'Rozanne', *Stachys byzantina* and *Nepeta* 'Six Hills Giant'.

Select plants for their interest: When choosing plants that embody the selected colours in your analogous scheme, remember that you don't have to focus just on their blooms; it could be their foliage, or even berries or fruit that fit the scheme.

From left to right: Scabiosa 'Black Knight', *Dahlia* 'Rocco', Sweet pea 'Just Jenny', *Geranium* 'Rozanne', Salvia 'Blue Queen', Sweet pea 'David Tostevin', Larkspur 'Fancy Picotee Purple', *Campanula* 'Loddon Anna', Nepeta 'Walker's Low', Sweet pea 'Ballerina Blue'

MONOCHROMATIC COLOURS

One of the most captivating ways to use colour in the garden is through a monochromatic scheme. When I say monochromatic, I don't mean black and white, but rather focusing on a single colour and exploring its full spectrum by layering up its tints, tones and shades. This approach creates a garden that feels soft, inviting and visually striking, while remaining cohesive and serene.

A monochromatic palette is particularly wonderful if you find yourself drawn to a specific colour. By working within a single hue, you can create an immersive, engaging space that highlights the richness and depth of the colour. Monochromatic gardens work beautifully because they focus on one colour, allowing the eye to rest while still offering variety through different tones, textures and forms. They can feel refined and intentional, yet they're simple to plan and execute because you can simply seek out plants in a single family of colour.

THE GOLDEN BORDER

For many years, I've tended to a monochromatic golden border, brimming with hues of yellow that ranged from creamy yellow to deep ochre. It all began with a gift from my father – 'Valencia', a bright yellow rose, which has sadly now gone out of cultivation. At first I thought the bold yellow would overwhelm, so I planted it by the compost heap to see how it would grow, and when it flowered, its soft golden-honey hue made my heart skip a beat. That single rose became the cornerstone of an entire golden garden.

I planned the border to begin with snowdrops in winter, followed by narcissi in spring. Then came the tulips 'Exotic Emperor' and *Tulipa sylvestris*, the buttery petals of this wild tulip unfolding like sunshine. Over time, the golden border has grown to include:

- 35 yellow and cream roses, including 'Valencia', 'Roald Dahl', 'Golden Celebration', 'Honey Dijon', 'Port Sunlight', 'Lichfield Angel' and 'Comte de Champagne'
- *Spiraea thunbergii*
- *Spiraea nipponica* 'Snowmound'
- *Magnolia stellata*
- *Filipendula ulmaria* (meadowsweet)
- *Cotinus coggygria* 'Golden Spirit'
- *Iris pseudacorus* (yellow flag iris)
- *Physocarpus opulifolius* 'Dart's Gold'
- *Digitalis purpurea albiflora*

To support the roses and combat blackspot (*Diplocarpon rosae*), a common fungal disease that affects roses, I recently introduced salvia as underplanting. While the addition of the blue salvias brought practical benefits, it slightly diluted the pure golden palette. If I were to redo this border, I'd likely opt for white salvias instead to retain the dazzling, gilded feel of the garden in its original monochromatic glory. Over time, the white foxgloves have sometimes reverted and introduced pink to the border too. It's now a whirlygig of colour, and though it's lost its monochromatic feeling, it is nothing but joyful.

DREAMING OF A PINK GARDEN

While my golden garden holds a special place in my heart, I also adore pink. For me, it's a colour that embodies playfulness and romance. Creating an entirely pink garden is on my list of future projects, and these are some of the plants I would include to explore the spectrum of pink hues:

Soft pastel tints: Pale pink roses, pink foxgloves and delicate *Astrantia major* 'Roma'

Vibrant tones: *Salvia nemorosa* 'Rose Queen', Dianthus 'Neon Star' and Peony 'Sarah Bernhardt'

Rich shades: Deep magenta Rosa 'Munstead Wood', *Persicaria bistorta* 'Superba' and Sedum 'Purple Emperor'

From left to right: Nigella 'Miss Jekyll White', White borage, *Agapanthus* 'Alba', Sweet pea 'Aphrodite', Rose 'Gentle Hermione' and 'Sexy Rexy', *Leucanthemum* 'Crazy Daisy', Gaura 'Whirling Butterflies', Sweet pea 'Keira Madeline', Snapdragon 'Appleblossom', Rose 'The Fairy', *Hydrangea arborescens* 'Pink Annabelle', *Malope* 'Vulcan', Rose 'Darcey Bussell', *Scabiosa* 'Black Knight'

COLOUR BIAS AND WARM AND COOL TONES

Our eye distinguishes warm colours as appearing to advance towards us, creating a sense of closeness and intensity. Conversely, cool colours can seem to recede, providing a calming and distant feel. Each colour on the wheel can contain a spectrum of warm to cool tones, even reds, which we think of as inherently warm, have cooler tones we can use (see the image on opposite page). This inherent warmth or coolness within colours is crucial in influencing our visual interpretation and emotional response to them, and it's to do with their underlying colour bias.

Colour bias refers to the tendency of a hue to lean away from the pure primary and towards a warmer or cooler aspect. We can describe these biased colours, for example, as 'orangey-red' or 'bluey-red', as a red with an orange undertone is warmer than one with a blue undertone. This indicates its shift in bias towards warmth or coolness. Recognizing the bias involves analysing hues to see if they suggest any temperature, whether warm or cool, by looking for other colours in its undertones.

With experience, this process becomes instinctive, and interpreting the temperature of colours gets easier. Developing the ability to read the undertones of colour is one of the most effective strategies to create a harmonious feel to a garden because choosing a palette dominated by either all warm or all cool colours is a shorthand way to help ensure colours work together seamlessly without clashing.

These images explore two sides of the spectrum; reds and pinks with warm undertones, and pinks with cool undertones. Shifts in temperature tone can completely change the mood and feel of a palette.

WARM TONES

Since the eye perceives warm toned colours (pictured below) as coming forward, we can use them in the garden to make the space feel more intimate. Warmer colours can make a garden feel welcoming and vibrant, especially when they are in full sun, which will make them become even more vivid.

From left to right: Rose 'Moka Rose' and 'Koko Loko', *Astilbe* 'Pretty in Pink', Poppy 'Pandora', Rose 'Darcey Bussell', *Dahlia* 'Burlesca', *Nasturtium* 'Ladybird Rose', Sweet pea 'Kings Ransom', *Heuchera* 'Marmalade', *Dahlia* 'Jowey Winnie', Rose 'Cinco de Mayo', Sweet pea 'Castlewellan', Malope 'Vulcan'

COOL TONES

Cool tones (pictured below) can feel a little more distant as our eye perceives them as receding, so we can use them in the garden to create more space for thinking and reflecting, creating a calmer, more meditative atmosphere.

From left to right: Rose 'Paul Transon', *Nicotiana* 'Marshmallow', *Geranium* 'Attar of Roses', *Sidalcea* 'Rosaly', Sweet pea 'Alisa', Clary sage 'Pink Lagoon', Rose 'The Generous Gardener', *Phlox* 'Ka-Pow Pink', Japanese anemone 'Robustissima', *Lavatera* 'Silver Blush', Sweet pea 'Bix'

PLACING COLOUR IN THE GARDEN

Using colour in beds and borders is one of the most powerful tools in garden design. When placed thoughtfully, colour can guide the eye, create movement and draw attention to specific areas of your garden. By strategically positioning drifts of colour, you can lead visitors along a path, highlight focal points or draw their gaze to something special, such as an entrance or water feature. Colour is my favouite way to add beauty, flow and mood to a space.

See more plant placement tips on page 87.

CREATING BALANCE WITH COLOUR

While colour can be exciting and dynamic, too much of it can overwhelm the senses. Balance is key. Think of colour as one piece of the design puzzle, working alongside texture and form to create harmony. Neutral textures and shapes – whether they come from soft foliage, architectural plants, or muted flowers – can calm and balance an intense colour scheme.

When selecting plants, consider their shapes and heights. A mix of spire-like, dotty and mound-shaped plants can create visual interest and help balance the border. This combination keeps your design from feeling chaotic while adding structure and depth.

BUILDING YOUR COLOUR PALETTE

If you're starting with an existing border, look at the plants you already love. Use them as the foundation for your colour palette, building complementary or contrasting tones around them. If a single plant feels out of place, consider whether it might work better elsewhere. Strong colours, for example, can sometimes feel overwhelming in large amounts, but using them as subtle accents can be just as impactful, especially in smaller gardens.

Tulip 'Angelique', *Viola* 'Nature Mulberry Shades'

If a clashing plant doesn't fit your vision, don't feel bad about relocating it. Research whether it might thrive in a container or a different part of your garden. Dig it up during its dormant period (usually winter), or take cuttings to preserve its beauty while integrating it more seamlessly into your space. You can always gift it to a friend who will love and tend to it.

YOUR GARDEN, YOUR COLOURS

Ultimately, colour in the garden is deeply personal. Some people love bold, intense clashes, while others prefer soft, harmonious tones. There's no right or wrong, only what feels right to you. If you adore bright, vibrant combinations, plant boldly and embrace the drama. If subtlety is more your style, focus on muted palettes with gentle contrasts. The beauty of gardening lies in its adaptability, and your garden should reflect your taste.

THE PLANTS

PULLING TOGETHER YOUR PLANT LIST

What's already there

If you're working with tweaking a mature border or an existing garden, begin gently by noticing and taking stock of what's already growing. Older shrubs and established trees are often the anchors of a space. They carry history, structure, and presence, and they're usually the most costly and time-consuming things to replace. So before rushing to remove or reimagine, take some time to really look.

You'll want to evaluate their health and placement. Could a tree benefit from some pruning to open up light for surrounding plants? Is there a shrub that could be relocated to better balance the border? If they're thriving and they fit your vision, you can work your new design around these existing features.

If you're starting fresh with a new border, look at what you already love growing elsewhere. If there's a plant you're fond of, consider propagating it. Many plants can be easily multiplied through cuttings, divisions or collecting seeds (see pages 144–63). This approach not only saves money but also adds a personal connection to your design.

Anemone hupehensis 'Queen Charlotte'

WHAT TO CONSIDER FOR A PLANT WISH LIST

Once you've assessed your garden's conditions and envisioned its future look, it's time to start researching plants that align with your site and style. Focus on plants suited to your specific conditions; sunlight levels, soil type and climate. For example:

North-facing border on heavy clay: Choose plants for part-shade and moisture-retentive soil, such as ferns, hostas or astilbe.

Sunny, free-draining soil: Look for drought-tolerant options, such as lavender, sedum or coneflowers.

Coastal gardens: Opt for salt-tolerant species, such as sea holly, thrift or grasses.

Plant labels (see page 86), nursery websites and gardening books are excellent resources for narrowing down your options of plants that will best suit your conditions.

MAKING YOUR WISH LIST

As you build your plant wish list, think beyond individual plants and consider the overall design. How will shapes, textures and colours interact? This is where your personal style comes into play. Each plant has its own personality, expressed through form, foliage, flowers and its growth habit. Spending time in gardens, both public and private, is one of the best ways to discover what resonates with you.

For a mixed border of any size, consider including a small tree, shrubs, perennials, bulbs, climbers and biennials/annuals.

RIGHT PLANT, RIGHT PLACE

Now that you've taken stock of your garden's unique conditions (soil type – see page 22, water distribution – see page 26, light exposure – see page 28), it's time to lean into what your site offers. While amending soil with organic matter can help, embracing the natural attributes of your space will guide you towards plants that thrive effortlessly. Observing where light falls and water pools, and how conditions change across your site, will inform your selections and help avoid future frustrations.

CONSIDER A PLANT'S MATURE SIZE

Don't forget to consider how large a plant will grow. Knowing its mature size will save you from overcrowding and reduce the need for constant pruning or transplanting later. Check plant labels, seed packets or reputable online resources for accurate height and spread information. Leaving enough space for each plant to thrive will lead to healthier, easier-to-maintain garden.

WHITTLING DOWN THE LIST

Now, if you're anything like me and greedy for plants, you probably have an extensive list of potential species, and far more than your space can accommodate. At this stage, it's a good idea to narrow down your selections to create a cohesive design that doesn't feel chaotic. Effective garden designs often feature a simple, limited palette of plants with the same varieties repeated throughout a border. This repetition brings harmony and allows the eye to move smoothly across the space. By contrast, having many single varieties forces the eye to jump around more, creating a disjointed and overwhelming effect.

However, this isn't a strict rule, as demonstrated by the beautiful, cohesive garden at the Serge Hill Project (see overleaf). It has hundreds of different plants, yet they have been thoughtfully grouped in swathes based on their needs, creating a natural extension of how plants grow in the wild.

When it comes to reducing your plant list, it involves continually evaluating plant attributes across different seasons. The final selections will be personal to you. For example, if I had to choose between a plant with a strong, sweet scent and one that flowers for a longer period, I would definitely prioritize the fragrance. Your priorities may differ, and that's where the joy lies – exploring endless combinations, making each garden uniquely reflect the individual who designed it.

A REMINDER TO KEEP YOUR LIST FLEXIBLE

One thing to keep in mind is that the ease of sourcing plants will vary depending on your location. Something that is widely available in one place, can be incredibly difficult or expensive to track down in another. The best advice I can offer on this is to keep your list flexible and remain open to substitutions where necessary.

THE SERGE HILL PROJECT – PLANT LIBRARY

One of the best ways to discover and connect with inspiring plants is to see them in person. Garden designer Tom Stuart-Smith and garden writer Sue Stuart-Smith have embarked on an exciting project at Serge Hill, Hertfordshire. They have established a Plant Library where visitors can explore how plants grow and behave within a garden setting. The Plant Library is accessible to members through a comprehensive database of more than 1,500 different varieties of primarily herbaceous plants. This makes the Plant Library a unique and extensive resource for education and ideal for anyone interested in plants and planting design. Situated on an acre of old orchard, the Plant Library organizes its collection in a systematic filing approach. Each plant group is assigned a QR code, allowing visitors to easily identify and learn about over 1,000 herbaceous plants and 400 varieties of bulbs.

I came away with a deeper appreciation for plant diversity… and a much longer wishlist of plants.

STILL STRUGGLING TO DECIDE?

Consult the chart on pages 77–83 to find plant recommendations based on soil type, pH levels and light needs.

Rose 'Roald Dahl'

KEY

☼ Full sun

☼ – ◑ Full sun to partial shade

◑ Partial shade

✿ Scented varieties

Scan the QR code to access the extended list of plant choices plus my personal favourite plant recommendations.

PLANT CHOICES AT A GLANCE

All-year interest

COMMON NAME	LATIN NAME	LIGHT LEVEL	SOIL PREFERENCE	PH PREFERENCE	PLANT TYPE	KEY NOTES
Bay laurel	*Laurus nobilis*	☼ – ◐	Loamy	Neutral	Evergreen shrub	Aromatic leaves for culinary use
Clematis	*Clematis*	☼ – ◐	Rich, well-drained	Neutral	Climber	Large showy flowers; requires sturdy support and routine pruning
Coral bells	*Heuchera*	◐	Loamy, moist	Neutral	Perennial	Colourful evergreen foliage, good for shade
Heavenly bamboo	*Nandina domestica*	☼ – ◐	Well-drained	Slightly acidic	Evergreen shrub	Red autumn foliage; bamboo-like, low maintenance
Hebe	*Hebe*	☼	Well-drained, dry	Neutral	Perennial, herbaceous	Unique, often architectural flower structures; some are toxic
Hornbeam	*Carpinus*	☼ – ◐	Loamy, clay	Various	Tree	Excellent hedge tree, retains brown leaves in winter
Ninebark	*Physocarpus*	☼ – ◐	Loamy, often slightly chalky	Alkaline	Shrub	Attractive exfoliating bark; low maintenance
❀ Oleaster	*Elaeagnus*	☼ – ◐	Sandy, loamy	Neutral	Evergreen shrub	Very tough and wind-tolerant; silvered leaves add interest
Yew	*Taxus*	☼ – ◐	Well-drained, loamy	Neutral	Evergreen tree	Dense, dark-green foliage; excellent for formal hedges or topiary

Spring interest

COMMON NAME	LATIN NAME	LIGHT LEVEL	SOIL PREFERENCE	PH PREFERENCE	PLANT TYPE	KEY NOTES
Avens	*Geum*	☼	Moist, well-drained	Neutral	Perennial	Bright flowers, good for borders
Bleeding hearts	*Dicentra*	◐	Rich, moist, well-drained	Neutral	Perennial	Heart-shaped, drooping flowers; shade-loving
Camassia	*Camassia leichtlinii*	☼ – ◐	Moist, well-drained	Neutral	Bulb	Blue spires of flowers; naturalistic planting
❀ Cherry	*Prunus*	☼	Loamy, well-drained	Neutral	Tree	Showy spring blossoms; edible fruit (varies by cultivar)
❀ Chocolate vine	*Akebia quinata*	◐	Well-drained	Neutral	Climber	Fragrant purple flowers, unusual edible fruit
Crocus	*Crocus*	☼ – ◐	Loamy, sandy	Neutral	Bulb	Early flowering, naturalizes well
❀ Daffodil	*Narcissus*	☼ – ◐	Loamy, well-drained	Neutral	Bulb	Classic trumpet-shaped spring flowers; naturalizes readily
Dwarf iris	*Iris reticulata*	☼	Well-drained, often rocky	Neutral to alkaline	Bulb, perennial	Early blooming; low-growing with vibrant colour
Fringecups	*Tellima grandiflora*	◐	Moist, humus-rich	Neutral	Perennial	Fringed green-white flowers, woodland plant
Garden angelica	*Angelica archangelica*	◐	Loamy	Neutral	Biennial	Tall, architectural; attracts pollinators
Granny's bonnet, Columbine	*Aquilegia*	☼ – ◐	Moist, well-drained	Neutral	Perennial	Delicate, nodding flowers; great for woodland edges

COMMON NAME	LATIN NAME	LIGHT LEVEL	SOIL PREFERENCE	PH PREFERENCE	PLANT TYPE	KEY NOTES
❀ Grape hyacinth	*Muscari*	☼	Well-drained, often rocky	Neutral	Bulb	Small clusters of blue blooms; naturalizes easily
❀ Honesty	*Lunaria annua*	◐	Moist, loamy	Neutral	Biennial	Silvery seed pods and magenta-purple blooms; ornamental seed display
❀ Juneberry	*Amelanchier*	☼ – ◐	Loamy	Neutral	Tree	White blossoms; notable autumn foliage; berries attract birds
❀ Magnolia	*Magnolia*	☼ – ◐	Rich, moist, well-drained	Slightly acidic	Deciduous tree	Large, fragrant blooms; impressive, showy flowers
Meadow rue	*Thalictrum*	☼ – ◐	Moist, well-drained, humus-rich	Neutral	Perennial	Airy foliage and clouds of delicate flowers; adds height and lightness to borders; supports pollinators
❀ Mexican orange blossom	*Choisya ternata*	☼ – ◐	Fertile, well-drained	Neutral	Evergreen shrub	Sweetly scented white flowers; excellent for hedges
Ornamental onion	*Allium*	☼	Loamy, well-drained	Neutral	Bulb	Pollinator-friendly, deer-resistant
Spiraea	*Spiraea*	☼ – ◐	Loamy	Neutral	Shrub	Compact habit; masses of small, delicate flowers
Summer snowflake	*Leucojum*	☼ – ◐	Moist, well-drained	Neutral	Bulb	Snowdrop-like white flowers; reliable spring bloomer
❀ Tulip	*Tulipa*	☼	Well-drained, often in clay pots	Neutral	Bulb	Iconic spring bloom; wide range of colours
❀ Wallflower	*Wallflower*	☼	Well-drained, moderately fertile	Neutral	Biennial, perennial	Fragrant and colourful; excellent for rock gardens
❀ Weigela	*Weigela*	☼	Loamy	Neutral	Shrub	Trumpet-shaped flowers attract hummingbirds

Summer interest

COMMON NAME	LATIN NAME	LIGHT LEVEL	SOIL PREFERENCE	PH PREFERENCE	PLANT TYPE	KEY NOTES
Aster	*Aster*	☼	Loamy, well-drained	Neutral	Perennial	Masses of blooms; late season interest; loved by pollinators
❀ Bearded iris	*Iris germanica*	☼	Rich, well-drained, moderate moisture	Neutral	Bulb	Bold blooms in early summer; needs sun & drainage; striking vertical form
Bellflower or canterbury bells	*Campanula*	☼ – ◐	Loamy	Neutral	Perennial	Delicate, bell-shaped flowers; excellent for naturalizing
Blueberry	*Vaccinium sect. Cyanococcus*	☼	Loamy, well-drained	Acidic to neutral	Annual	Loves moisture & acidity; good fruit; supports wildlife
❀ Bronze fennel	*Foeniculum vulgare*	☼	Loamy, well-drained	Neutral	Perennial	Fine, feathery foliage; aromatic; good for pollinators
Bugbane	*Actaea*	◐	Moist, rich	Neutral	Perennial	Mounded habit; attractive, airy flower clusters
❀ Catmint	*Nepeta*	☼ – ◐	Loamy, sometimes chalky	Alkaline	Perennial	Low maintenance; drought-tolerant; attracts bees
Coneflower	*Echinacea*	☼	Fertile, well-drained	Neutral	Tuberous perennial	Long flowering; attract pollinators; excellent for late-summer colour
Deutzia	*Deutzia*	☼ – ◐	Loamy	Neutral	Shrub	Showy clusters; low maintenance
Fleabane	*Erigeron karvinskianus*	☼	Sandy, well-drained	Neutral	Biennial	Spreading daisy-like flowers; thrives in poor soil; blooms for month
Foxglove	*Digitalis grandiflora*	◐	Well-drained, humus-rich	Neutral	Biennial, perennial	Tall, tubular spikes; attracts pollinators, can be invasive
Gentian speedwell	*Veronica gentianoides*	☼	Loamy	Slightly acidic	Shrub	Low-growing, pale blu flowers; ideal for rockeries or edging
Giant hyssop	*Agastache*	☼	Well-drained	Neutral	Perennial	Aromatic leaves; long-lasting flower spikes; excellent for pollinators
Giant scabious	*Cephalaria tatarica*	☼	Acidic, well-drained	Acidic	Shrub	Large pale flowers on tall stems; attracts bees bold border impact

COMMON NAME	LATIN NAME	LIGHT LEVEL	SOIL PREFERENCE	PH PREFERENCE	PLANT TYPE	KEY NOTES
Hydrangea	*Hydrangea paniculata*	☼ – ◐	Rich, moist, well-drained	Slightly acidic	Shrub	Large cone-shaped clusters; long season of interest
Japanese anemone	*Anemone hupehensis*	◐	Moist, rich, well-drained	Neutral	Perennial	Elegant, drooping flowers; excellent for mixing in shade
Knotweed	*Persicaria*	☼ – ◐	Moist, well-drained	Neutral	Perennial	Spikes of small flowers, long blooming
❀ Lavender	*Lavandula*	☼	Rich, well-drained	Neutral	Biennial, perennial	Scented silver foliage; drought-tolerant; excellent for pollinators
❀ Lupine	*Lupin*	☼	Well-drained, loamy	Neutral to alkaline	Bulb, perennial	Bold spires of colour; cottage classic; enriches soil with nitrogen
Martagon lily	*Lilium martagon*	◐	Rich, well-drained	Neutral	Bulb	Turk's cap type with recurved petals; woodland plant
Masterwort	*Astrantia*	◐	Loamy	Neutral	Perennial	Long-blooming; great for cutting, bouquets
❀ Meadowsweet	*Filipendula rubra*	☼ – ◐	Rich, moist	Neutral	Perennial shrub	Fragrant, airy clusters; attractive to pollinators
Plume thistle	*Cirsium rivulare*	☼	Loamy, well-drained	Slightly alkaline or slightly acidic or neutral	Perennial, annual	Fluffy plumes; loved by pollinators; tall and architectural
Prairie mallow	*Sidalcea*	☼	Moist, well-drained	Neutral	Perennial grass	Light and airy habit; good for movement
❀ Rose	*Rosa*	☼	Loamy, well-drained	Neutral	Annual climber	Many varieties scented and repeat flowering
❀ Salvia	*Salvia*	☼	Loamy, well-drained	Neutral	Perennial	Long blooming; pollinator magnet
Smoke Bush	*Cotinus coggygria*	☼	Loamy	Neutral	Annual	Fluffy floral plumes
❀ Star jasmine	*Trachelospermum*	☼ – ◐	Well-drained	Neutral	Climber	Evergreen, fragrant star-shaped flowers
Turkish sage	*Phlomis russeliana*	☼	Well-drained	Neutral	Perennial	Evergreen leaves, great seed heads
Vervain	*Verbena bonariensis*	☼	Loamy	Neutral to alkaline	Perennial	Tall, airy stems, long season
Vervain	*Verbena hastata*	☼	Loamy, well-drained	Neutral to slightly acidic	Shrub, climber	Tall, airy spires, long flowering; attracts pollinators

Autumn interest

COMMON NAME	LATIN NAME	LIGHT LEVEL	SOIL PREFERENCE	PH PREFERENCE	PLANT TYPE	KEY NOTES
Acer or sometimes maple	*Acer*	☼ – ◐	Moist, well-drained	Slightly acidic	Tree	Iconic autumn colour; various sizes and forms
❀ Apple	*Malus*	☼	Loamy	Neutral	Tree	Fruit-bearing; spring blossoms
Black-eyed Susan	*Rudbeckia*	☼	Loamy	Neutral	Perennial	Bold yellow daisy-like flowers; late blooming
Katsura	*Cercidiphyllum japonicum*	☼ – ◐	Moist, well-drained	Neutral	Deciduous tree	Heart-shaped leaves with sweet, caramel-like scent; striking autumn colour
Mums or chrysanthus	*Chrysanthemum*	☼	Well-drained	Neutral	Perennial, annual	Classic autumn blooms; great for seasonal displays
❀ Nerine	*Nerine*	☼	Sandy, well-drained	Neutral to alkaline	Bulb	Frilly, bright flowers; often used in container gardens
Oak	*Quercus*	☼ – ◐	Well-drained, loamy	Neutral	Tree	Stately hardwood; supports a wide variety of wildlife
Sedum	*Hylotelephium*	☼	Sandy, loamy	Neutral	Perennial, succulent	Very drought tolerant; large, clustering flower heads

Winter interest

COMMON NAME	LATIN NAME	LIGHT LEVEL	SOIL PREFERENCE	PH PREFERENCE	PLANT TYPE	KEY NOTES
Camellia	*Camellia japonica*	◑	Acidic, well-drained	Acidic	Evergreen shrub	Glossy evergreen leaves; showy, long-lasting blooms
❁ Daphne	*Daphne*	◑	Fertile, well-drained	Neutral	Evergreen shrub	Intensely fragrant winter–spring blooms; attractive glossy leaves
Lenten rose or hellebore	*Helleborus*	◑	Clay, chalky	Acidic	Evergreen perennial	Tough foliage; blooms very early in winter into spring
❁ Mahonia	*Mahonia*	☼ – ◑	Clay	Acidic	Evergreen shrub	Spring leaves; yellow flowers and blue berries; attracts birds
Silktassel bush	*Garrya elliptica*	☼ – ◑	Well-drained	Neutral	Evergreen shrub	Silvery tassels in winter; low maintenance
Snowberry	*Symphoricarpos*	☼ – ◑	Loamy, well-drained	Neutral	Deciduous shrub	White, persistent berries; used as screening
Snowdrop	*Galanthus*	◑	Moist, well-drained	Neutral	Bulb	Early blooming woodland plant
❁ Winter honeysuckle	*Lonicera fragrantissima*	☼ – ◑	Loamy	Neutral	Semi-evergreen shrub	Intensely fragrant flowers; blooms on bare stems
❁ Wintersweet	*Chimonanthus praecox*	☼ – ◑	Sandy, loamy	Slightly acidic	Deciduous shrub	Highly fragrant winter blooms
❁ Viburnum	*Viburnum*	◑	Loamy	Neutral	Shrub; some species evergreen	Fragrant blooms; many species offer both ornamental and wildlife interest

WORKING OUT HOW MANY PLANTS YOU NEED

Whatever the size of your border, be it a tiny strip or a large swathe of a bed, you will need to calculate its area. Knowing how many square metres (or square feet) your border contains will better help you to calculate the number of plants you need to fill it.

To calculate your border's area, use a long tape measure or pace out the dimensions to find the length and width, then apply the area formula (A = W x L). For a rectangular or square border, simply multiply length by width. If your border is an irregular shape, break it into smaller rectangles or squares, calculate each area, and then add them together.

Once you know how much space you're working with, take a moment to think about the plants you've chosen and how they'll grow over time. Will they need room to spread? Could they crowd one another out? Planning with their mature size in mind means less upheaval later. You can always tuck in smaller, faster-growing filler plants, like annuals or biennials, to bring beauty and colour while slower perennials find their feet. I find planting in the gaps also helps with weed suppression. If you'd like help shaping your planting placements, turn to page 89 for a simple guide to layering, balance and rhythm.

RATIOS OF PLANTS

As a general rule when choosing ratios of different plants, the bigger the scale of the plant, the fewer you'll need. This illustration below is just a visual guide, so there is no hard and fast rule here. As you move down this triangle; the plant size gets smaller and smaller, so you can add more of those plant types to your design.

PLANTS PER LAYER

(based on a border size (3.5 x 2 metre/11½ x 6½ feet)

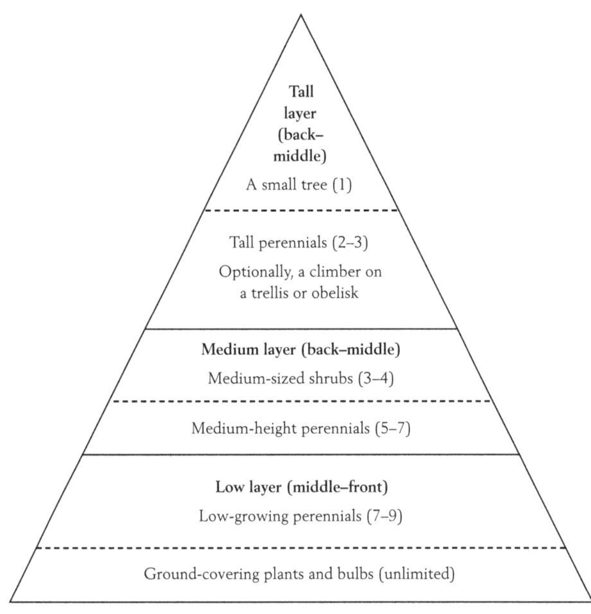

SOURCING PLANTS

I love sourcing plants; it's one of my favourite parts of gardening. Once I fall head over heels for a particular plant variety, I relish the thrill of the hunt to find it. Whether you're seeking seeds, plugs or mature plants, there are many ways to bring your wish list to life. Remember, there are multiple choices, so if you can't track down a particular variety, there will likely be a suitable substitute out there.

Mail-order nurseries are a treasure trove for sourcing plants, offering a vast range of varieties that might not be available locally. But don't overlook what's already close to home. Ask friends or family if they grow the plants you're after, they might share a cutting or some seeds. Using plants from loved ones' gardens (or even your own) is also a cost-effective and lovely way of connecting your garden with meaningful memories.

A NOTE ON PLANT SIZES

I'm a strong advocate for growing plants from seeds, divisions, and cuttings. However, when I do source plants from elsewhere, I almost always choose perennials in 9-cm (3½-inch) pots. I find that plants establish more easily and adapt better to my garden when they start from this size, rather than those sold in larger 17-cm (6½-inch) pots.

That said, there are some exceptions, especially with shrubs. In most cases, I prefer to buy the most mature shrubs my budget allows. However, many fast-growing varieties will reach their full size within a few years. For example, I planted a row of *Hebe parviflora angustifolia* in 5-litre pots, and within just a few years, they've grown into an impressive hedge 22.5 cm (6 feet) tall.

When it comes to trees, I opt for whips – young trees around 2–4 years old. They establish well and tend to grow quickly. However, if you're looking for more immediate impact and don't plan to stay in your garden long-term, investing in a mature tree may be worthwhile, although it can be costly to buy and have delivered.

PURCHASING PLANTS IN PERSON

If you prefer to shop locally, visiting a nursery gives you the chance to inspect plants up close and ensure you're choosing healthy specimens. Here are some tips for selecting the best.

Check the leaves: Look for vibrant, healthy foliage. Avoid plants with yellowing, browning or wilting leaves, although in autumn this rule can be relaxed as plants begin their natural seasonal decline.

Inspect for unwelcome features: Examine leaves and soil for signs of trouble, such as webs, holes or sticky residue.

Assess stems: Opt for plants with strong, sturdy stems and avoid those that look floppy or weak.

Inspect the roots: If possible, gently slide the plant out of its pot to check for root health. Avoid root-bound plants – those with tightly wound, overcrowded roots that can limit growth. Signs include roots visible at the bottom of the pot, or plants that slip out of their containers too easily.

Small is often better: Small plants tend to adapt more easily and establish better than larger ones. They grow into their space more naturally, often catching up to or surpassing larger plants over time.

Choose pleasing forms: Shopping in person allows you to select plants with the most attractive shapes and growth habits.

Look for buds, not blooms: Plants that are in full bloom are, of course the most tempting to purchase. However, as they are peaking at their flowering time, they are expending the most energy, which means they are the more likely to struggle to settle in once planted.

UNDERSTANDING A PLANT LABEL

Plant labels can be a great source of information that can help you choose the right plant for your garden and ensure it thrives. Here's a breakdown of the key elements you'll find on a plant label and what they mean:

SUN, SHADE OR PARTIAL SHADE REQUIREMENTS

This tells you how much sunlight the plant needs to thrive.

Full sun: The plant needs more than 6 hours of direct sunlight per day during midsummer. **Examples:** sunflowers, lavender, tomatoes.

Part shade: The plant requires 3–6 hours of direct sunlight per day during midsummer. **Examples:** ferns, foxgloves, hydrangeas.

Full shade: The plant tolerates less than 2–3 hours of direct sunlight per day. Perfect for areas under tree canopies or along shaded walls. **Examples:** hostas, hellebores.

Deep shade: The plant can survive in less than 2 hours of direct sunlight per day, often under dense trees or in areas with heavy overhangs. **Examples:** ferns, ivy.

HARDINESS ZONE

When 'zoning' is used to describe a plant's hardiness, it refers to climate zones and a plant's tolerance for different temperatures. This is different from how 'zoning' is used in garden design, where it means dividing a space into functional areas (see page 44). Zoning for hardiness is intended primarily for the USA. Look for the zone number on the label (e.g. zones 5–8). Check this against your local zone to ensure the plant can survive in your climate:

Zone 3 means the plant can withstand very cold winters (-40°F/-40°C).

Zone 10 means the plant prefers warmer climates and won't tolerate frost.

SIZE AT MATURITY

This tells you how tall the plant will grow when fully mature. The label might also indicate spread, which tells you the width it will reach. This is helpful for spacing plants to prevent overcrowding.

MOISTURE AND DRAINAGE NEEDS

These details help you to understand the plant's water and soil preferences.

Well-drained soil: The plant doesn't like to sit in waterlogged soil. **Examples:** lavender, succulents.

Moist but well-drained soil: The plant enjoys consistent moisture but hates standing water. **Examples:** peonies, roses.

Wet or boggy soil: The plant thrives in areas that stay damp, such as waterlogged areas and the edges of ponds. **Examples:** flag iris, marsh marigolds.

PLANT PLACEMENT PLAN

This is a good moment to double-check the plant quantities you'll need and to start thinking about possible placements of each plant in your overall design. You can start from the initial plan you drew during the zone mapping exercise (see page 43), or you can start from scratch if you want to hone in on the border alone.

You will need

- Pen/pencil
- Graph paper
- Tracing paper

Step By Step

1. DRAW YOUR BORDER
Use graph paper to sketch your border, scaling it to size by using the squares as measurements (e.g. 1 square = 1 metre (3 feet). This will give you a manageable, accurate layout to work from.

2. GATHER PLANT SIZES
Look up the approximate mature size and spread of your chosen plants. This information is usually available on plant labels, online, or in reference books. If you plan to prune some plants to a smaller size, use their maintained size for your plan.

3. LAYER WITH TRACING PAPER
Use tracing paper to add layers of planting to your border design. Start with a base layer for structural plantings like evergreen shrubs and trees, and then overlay additional layers to map out herbaceous perennials, bulbs or other plants (see page 84).

4. ESTIMATE PLANT QUANTITIES
As a general approximation: 1 square metre (11 square feet) fits approximately 5 herbaceous perennials, 3 small shrubs or 1 large shrub. Bulbs can be layered throughout and beneath perennials for seasonal interest.

5. PLACE STRUCTURAL PLANTS FIRST
Choose potential positions for evergreen and large structural plants first. These form the 'bones' of your border, providing year-round interest and a sense of permanence.

6. GROUP PERENNIALS AND SHRUBS
Add herbaceous perennials or small deciduous shrubs in groups of the same species or cultivar. Aim to use odd numbers (e.g. groups of 3 or 5) to avoid a 'spotty' look. Repeat these groups along the border to create flow and unity in the design.

7. POSITION BY HEIGHT
Place the tallest and most substantial plants towards the back of the border. For added depth and a natural look, include tall, slender plants or those with airy canopies near the front to create layers of interest.

PLANT PLACEMENT TIPS

As you think about where each plant might go in your design, it is a good moment to double check the quantities you need (see page 84 for help with plant quantities). You can start trying placements out on your original zone map or sketch something new, but keep it flexible as plans often change once you're on the ground and can see the plants in place. Placement is one of the most important steps in making a garden; how plants speak to each other, guide the eye, and invite you in will shape the whole space. There's no need to rush planting once you've got your plants, so long as they're watered, let new plants sit nearby while you watch the light, notice the day's movement, and trust your instincts to find them the right home. Here are some key principles and techniques to help you achieve balance, flow and depth in your garden design.

REPETITION

Grouping clusters of the same plant and repeating them throughout the border or across the whole of your plot. Repetition is one of the easiest ways to create unity and cohesion in your garden. It will make your space feel harmonious and intentional. Alternatively, you can use plants with similar colours or textures to achieve a subtler sense of repetition.

Repeating the same plant in drifts or clusters enhances the visual impact of a particular colour or texture but also adds rhythm to your design. Rhythm encourages the eye to move naturally across the space, helping you to visually interpret depth and flow within the border.

Try this: Repeat the same plants in clusters. Try choosing the same sorts of plants not just in one border, but have some repeat through others. For example, I repeat *Pittosporum tenuifolium* (an evergreen shrub with many different varieties – see image opposite) through the different parts of my garden and it acts like a thread, connecting one border to another.

SCALE

Understanding the scale of plants is essential for a balanced and proportionate design. Overwhelming a small garden with large trees can feel cramped, while a single, well-placed small tree can open up the space and make it feel larger.

Think about how scale can create balance. For instance, a small tree could be paired with medium-sized shrubs and an underplanting of smaller perennials. This layering creates a sense of harmony and ensures no single element dominates the design.

Try this: Use one larger feature, like a small tree, to anchor the space and balance it by underplanting the space below and around it with medium and smaller plants of varying heights and widths.

FLOW

Guiding the eye through the garden and creating a sense of movement is called flow. Position plants in soft, river-like waves to form gentle drifts. Repeating plants across different parts of the border, and even across other borders, will enhance the overall flow and tie your garden together.

Try this: Choose perennials with similar colours, such as *Nepeta* 'Walker's Low' and lavender 'Munstead', and repeat them throughout your garden to create a sense of movement or connection so that the design flows smoothly and naturally from one area to the next, just as a river winds through the landscape. When these plants bloom together, their colour will create a unifying, effect through the space.

White foxgloves, Apple tree 'Katy', *Pittosporum tenuifolim* 'Golf Ball'

DEPTH

Creating depth adds dimension and dynamism to your garden, making it more engaging to look at. One way to create depth is by staggering plants instead of lining them up. Nature rarely arranges plants in neat rows, so staggering mimics the natural feel of a wild landscape.

Try this: Arrange plants in staggered lines, placing some in front of or behind others. This not only looks more natural but also helps make smaller spaces feel larger.

LAYERING

This technique involves arranging plants of different heights to create a rich, dimensional landscape. Imagine your garden as a multi-layered cake, with each layer adding its own flavour and texture.

Top layer (canopy): Tall trees or small trees 'borrowed' from the landscape beyond your garden.

Understory: Smaller trees and tall shrubs.

Shrub layer: Medium-sized plants that add structure and form.

Herbaceous layer: Perennials that provide seasonal colour and movement.

Ground cover: Low-growing plants that hug the soil and fill in gaps.

To create a classic layered effect, place tall plants at the back of a border and shorter ones at the front. However, for a more dynamic and playful design, mix heights throughout. For example, tall alliums can meander from the back to the front of the border, or a small, open-growing tree, such as hazel, can be positioned in the middle of a bed, offering glimpses through its branches.

Try this: Use multi-stemmed trees, such as *Viburnum x bodnantense* or coppiced hazel to create interest in the middle layer, or weave tall bulbs, such as alliums, through the entire border for a whimsical touch.

HOW TO PREPARE A BORDER FROM SCRATCH

When making brand new borders, the method I favour involves no-digging. You can plant straight into a newly made no-dig bed, and is great to use across all soil types, particularly heavy clay which is a much harder to dig over. If you have access to a good amount of compost, it can be a quick and environmentally friendly way to transform your garden space. By following these steps, you'll have a beautiful, productive garden bed ready to plant with minimal effort. If access to compost is more of a challenge, then dig over the bed thoroughly with a fork and spade, removing any turf as you go.

To maintain a no-dig bed keep removing weeds as they come up and once a year top up the organic mulch by a few cm.

A NOTE ON BED/BORDER SIZE

I prefer a deep border of at least 1 metre (3 feet) to achieve a layered planting layout (see page 89 for layering planting tips). This depth allows for more dynamic design, giving plants space to grow while guiding the viewer's eye through the composition.

The size of your bed or border ultimately comes down to personal preference and the space you have available. However, I encourage you to be generous: designing a well-balanced and visually appealing planting scheme is much easier when you have plenty of room to work with.

You will need:

- **Stakes:** To mark out your border's size and shape
- **Rope or string:** Secured around the stakes, this helps to mark the edge of your new border
- **Lawn mower (optional):** For cutting the grass
- **Trowel or hori hori:** For digging out perennial weeds
- **Cardboard:** Thick, untreated cardboard to suppress weeds and act as a barrier
- **Watering can or hosepipe:** To water the cardboard and plants thoroughly
- **Wheelbarrow (optional):** To transport compost and plants
- **High-quality compost or well-rotted organic matter:** Enough to spread to a depth of 7.5–12.5 cm (3–5 inches). There are some good online compost calculators to help work out how much you'll need:
- **Rake (optional):** To smooth out the compost
- **Spade:** For planting
- **Plants:** A selection of plants suited to your border design and garden conditions
- **Half-moon turf cutter or flat-backed spade:** For creating neat edges

1. MARK THE BORDER

Place your stakes in the ground at intervals to mark out your bed. Tie rope or string around the stakes to outline the edges of your border. This ensures a clean, defined area to work with.

2. PREPARE THE AREA

If your border is being created within a grassy area, mow the grass as short as possible. Dig out deep taproots of any persistent perennial weeds, such as dandelions or dock, to prevent regrowth.

3. ADD A LAYER OF CARDBOARD

Spread thick, untreated cardboard over the entire area, ensuring there are no gaps. The cardboard will suppress weeds and decompose over time. Make sure there is no plastic tape on the cardboard and remove any stickers to the best of your ability. Wet the cardboard lightly with a watering can or hosepipe. This helps it break down and stay in place. If preferred, you can use a turf cutter to flip the top layer of grass upside down within the border area before adding the cardboard and compost. This approach allows the grass to rot down, contributing to the organic matter in the soil.

4. ADD COMPOST

Spread compost or well-rotted organic matter to an even depth of 7.5–12.5 cm (3–5 inches) over the cardboard. This layer provides nutrients and acts as the growing medium for your plants. Smooth it out with a rake or your hands.

5. SET OUT YOUR PLANTS

Before you start digging, sit your plants, still in their pots, on the soil in a rough approximation of your design. Remember these design tips:

Group in odd numbers: Use clusters of three, five or seven for a more natural, harmonious look.

Create repetition: Repeat the same plant or colour throughout the border to create rhythm and cohesion.

Don't worry if it doesn't look perfect as this is your chance to get a sense of spacing and flow and move things around before committing. Step back and view the layout from different angles to ensure it feels balanced and visually appealing.

6. SPACING

Give plants enough room to reach their full size, but aim for a full, abundant border where bare soil is hidden during summer. I plant based on the approximate mature size and spread, leaving minimal extra space. However, if you live in a humid climate or an area prone to disease, consider slightly wider spacing to improve airflow.

Clockwise from top left: Anthriscus sylvestris 'Ravenswing', *Aquilegia* 'Nora Barlow', *Digitalis purpurea* 'Alba', *Geranium* 'Rebecca Moss', Hellebore 'Ice 'n' Roses', *Heuchera* 'Apple Crisp', *Linaria* 'Springside White', *Malva moschata* 'Alba', *Nepeta mussinii* 'Alba', *Pittosporum* 'Golf Ball' and 'Tom Thumb', *Sidalcea* 'Rosaly', Apple tree 'Katy'

7. PLANTING

When happy with your layout, dig holes through the compost and cardboard into the ground beneath for each plant. Gently remove the plants from their pots and place them in their holes, backfill with compost and firm the soil around them. Water each plant thoroughly to help it settle in.

8. EDGE THE BORDER

For a neat finish, use a half-moon turf cutter or a flat-backed spade to cut clean edges around your border.

The new border 6 months later, and a border of my favourite north facing tolerant rose: Olivia Rose Austen

HOW TO TWEAK AN EXISTING BORDER

Whether you've inherited a garden that you want to make your own, are renovating to create a new look, or simply want to restore balance to a mature border that has developed seasonal gaps or become unruly, every border benefits from a good assessment now and then. A refresh can breathe new life into your garden and ensure it continues to thrive and delight.

While autumn is the ideal time to undertake this process (plants are becoming dormant but still have time to establish before winter), spring is also a great time for tweaking a border. In spring, plants are actively growing, making it easier to see which ones need moving or dividing and where gaps need filling.

You will need:

- **Spade:** For planting
- **Pots:** Or somewhere to place plants you dig up
- **Hoe:** for removing annual weeds
- **Trowel or hori hori:** For digging out perennial weeds
- **Wheelbarrow (optional):** To transport compost and plants
- **Plants:** A selection of plants suited to your border design and garden conditions
- **Watering can or hosepipe:** To water the bed and plants thoroughly
- **High-quality compost or well-rotted organic matter:** Enough to spread to a depth of 2.5–5 cm (1–2 inches). There are some good online compost calculators to help work out how much you'll need

1. EVALUATE THE BORDER
Take a moment to step back and assess your border. Does it feel balanced? Are there plants that have outgrown their space or are dominating others? Do you notice seasonal gaps or areas where interest fades at certain times of the year? Identify which plants you love and want to keep, and which ones no longer serve your vision.

2. REMOVE UNWANTED PLANTS
Carefully dig up any plants you no longer want in the border. Remove the entire root ball to prevent regrowth. Pot them up to move elsewhere in the garden, gift them to friends or compost them if they're not needed.

3. PROPAGATE YOUR FAVOURITES
Take the opportunity to propagate plants you want more of. Split large, established plants into smaller sections – larger divisions can be replanted directly, while smaller ones should be potted up and nurtured until they are ready for planting out (usually when the roots fill a 9-cm/3½-inch pot).

To take cuttings, propagate from healthy stems (see page 156).

4. PREPARE THE GROUND
Remove any weeds from the border. Use a hoe for annual weeds, and a trowel or hori hori knife for digging out perennial weeds and their taproots. Clear any debris or piles of fallen leaves to make the task of placing plants in their pots easier (add the debris to your compost heap, but if your heap doesn't get very hot, be sure to remove any leaves with signs of disease before composting and dispose of them separately).

5. PLACE YOUR REPLACEMENT PLANTS
Arrange your new plants, considering their mature sizes and how they'll work with the remaining plants. Step back and view the layout from multiple angles to ensure a balanced, pleasing design. Don't rush – this is your chance to tweak and adjust until it feels just right.

6. PLANT THE REPLACEMENTS
Dig a hole for each plant, making it wide and deep enough for the root ball. Gently remove the plant from its pot, tease out any compacted roots and place it in the hole. Backfill with soil, firming it gently around the base, and water thoroughly to settle the plant in.

7. TOP UP WITH COMPOST
Spread a 2.5–5-cm (1–2-inch) layer of compost across the entire bed. This mulch will enrich the soil, retain moisture and suppress weeds, giving your plants the best start. No need to dig it in as the earthworms and microbes will incorporate it for you. You can also use topsoil instead, if your plants require a less nutrient-dense mulch.

CONTAINER GARDENING

Embarking on container gardening is an excellent way to enjoy plants without the need for extensive garden space or direct access to the earth. Whether you're working with a balcony, patio or even an indoor area, container gardens offer flexibility and beauty throughout the year. My first gardens were in pots dragged from flatshare to flatshare. The constant failures I had with them led me to believe I was not in the possession of a green thumb; and I had avoided pots for a long while. My business partner Paris gardens in containers at home in a courtyard garden. She has created a transformative oasis, filled with shady nooks, cut flowers, and vegetables; it is an inspiring place to sit. Over the last few years, she has really encouraged me to think differently about growing in pots and got me to try them again; I have to say, I have enjoyed the journey immensely.

The principles we've already talked through, from colour to layering plants, can still apply; if you think of it as a 'border in moveable pieces', it can suddenly become a really fun and adaptable way of gardening.

CHOOSING THE RIGHT CONTAINER

Variety in pot sizes: Start by selecting an assortment of pot sizes to add depth and interest to your garden. I like to incorporate at least one extra-large container as a statement piece. As a general rule, I say get the biggest pots you can that will fit well in your space – they are much easier to maintain as they hold water and nutrients more effectively than small pots. During hot weather especially, small pots need almost constant watering to avoid drying out.

A variety of sizes not only enhances the visual appeal, but also allows you to accommodate different plant sizes and root systems effectively. To create even more varying heights, you can use bricks or an upside-down pot to elevate certain containers. I love this approach as I find it such a joy to rearrange my garden in pots as the season progresses, giving me the chance to showcase different plants as they come into focus through the ever changing months. For example, adding height to small pots filled with spring-flowering bulbs brings delicate details closer to the eyeline when they're in bloom.

Grouping for flexibility: Instead of a few large pots dotted around, I like to group my pots together to create a 'garden border' look. This strategy can also maximize seasonal interest and keeps your garden dynamic, as it facilitates the easy swapping around of pots and plants. For instance, you can easily lift spring bulbs from a pot once they're over and replace them with summer annuals without disrupting the overall arrangement.

Container materials: I love a beautiful clay pot, but plastic has lower transpiration rates compared to terracotta, helping to retain moisture and reducing the frequency of watering. Consider placing plastic containers inside decorative outer pots, as it can allow you to interchange plants easily while maintaining a lovely, polished arrangement. If you want a stylish look on a budget, place terracotta or metal pots at the front of your grouping and have plastic containers at the back. This approach allows you to use functional, cost-effective pots without compromising the garden's overall appearance.

Also see page 104 for a container garden recipe.

Opposite: Muscari 'Valerie Finnis' and forced narciss in a winter container garden

PREPARING THE CONTAINERS

Layering for optimized growth: You don't need to fill extra-large pots entirely with compost, especially when planting annuals, herbaceous perennials or plants with short root systems. Instead, create a layered base to promote drainage and provide a foundation for your plants.

Drainage layer: Place large stones, broken pieces of crockery or gravel at the bottom of your pots. This layer ensures excess water can escape and avoids root rot.

Organic matter: If there's a lot of room to fill and you don't want to spend too much money and effort on speciality container compost, you can add a layer of collected fallen leaves or partially composted material on top of the stones. This not only improves drainage but also gradually breaks down to enrich the soil over time.

When to use quality compost: If you plan to plant large shrubs or small trees, it's advisable to fill the container with high-quality compost. Large plants have more extensive root systems and higher nutrient requirements, so rich soil will support their growth and longevity. You might need to re-pot your tree into a bigger pot as it grows. Alternatively, choose a variety that won't grow too large and top up each year with rich compost.

CONTAINER PLANTS FOR YEAR-ROUND APPEAL

Evergreen shrubs and perennials: Incorporate evergreen shrubs, like my personal favourite for use in borders, *Pittosporum tennuifolium*, to maintain structure and greenery throughout the year. Smaller plants such as heucheras offer vibrant foliage that adds colour and texture even in colder months.

Seasonal colour with bulbs and annuals: To ensure your container garden remains colourful during less vibrant times of the year, tuck in bulbs, such as tulips or daffodils. These bulbs bloom in spring and add a splash of colour after winter. In the warmer months, swap bulbs with annuals, such as cosmos or violas, to maintain continuous bloom.

Small trees for structure and interest: Choose a compact tree, one that blossoms in spring and showcases colourful foliage or fruit in autumn is particularly lovely for seasonal interest. A tree is such a great way to add vertical interest and serves as a focal point within your container garden.

MAINTENANCE TIPS

Regular plant swapping: Maximize seasonal interest by regularly replacing annuals with bulbs during transitional periods to keep the garden lively and colourful throughout the year. Plant spring-flowering bulbs in autumn and sow summer-flowering annuals in spring.

Ease of interchange: Using small plastic tubs within large decorative pots makes swapping plants effortless and allows you to experiment with different plant combinations.

Watering and nutrient management: Ensure that all containers have proper drainage to prevent waterlogging. Depending on the plant types, water consistently to keep the soil moist but not soggy. For larger shrubs or trees, replenish the compost periodically to maintain nutrient levels.

Also see page 105 for more on container care.

From left to right: Euphorbia 'Miners Merlot', *Physocarpus* 'Amber Queen', *Pittosporum* 'Gold Ball', *Malus* 'Royalty', Cosmos 'Xanthos', *Nemesia* 'Wisley Vanilla'

Clockwise from top right: Pittosporum 'Silver Queen', *Narcissus* 'Thalia', Rose 'Desdemona', Hellebore 'Double Ellen Purple', *Helleborus foetidus,* tubs of tulips 'Pink Mix'

GARDEN RECIPES

Simple ideas for your space

The suggestions given in this section are inspired by the tried-and-tested plantings in my own garden, which have flourished and matured beautifully over time. They've proven to work wonderfully, providing a reliable foundation for gardening success. Feel free to personalize them by swapping out varieties to better suit your specific conditions and personal tastes.

ALLOWING FOR SPONTANEITY

One of the most pleasing things about gardening is when plants put themselves in places I would never think of. My very favourite plant combinations have been born this way. When a new border is planted, the plants will take time to mature. During the first few years, when shrubs and perennials are still growing into the space, there will be plenty of gaps. Allow these to be an opportunity for spontaneity. Every spring, I scatter aquilegia and foxglove seed heads throughout the garden, hoping they'll find new homes to bloom in unexpected places. It's a joyful way to invite a bit of wildness and surprise into the borders, ensuring the garden always feels alive and full of character.

Sometimes I will even plan gaps into the border, leaving spaces that will remain 3–5 small gaps even after the border has grown to maturity. These spaces, each about 30–45 cm (12–15 inches) in diameter, allow nature to take the lead. They become opportunities for self-seeding plants, such as foxgloves, wallflowers and sweet rocket, to settle and germinate. They can also be used for plugging in summer annuals, such as cosmos.

Opposite: Autumn container garden containing, *Malus* (crab apple) 'Royalty', *Pittosporum* 'Golf Ball', Katsura tree, *Physocarpus* 'Amber Queen', Physocarpus 'Panther', *Euphorbia* 'Miners Merlot', Pansies 'Rose Blotch', *Heuchera* 'Marmalade' and 'Blackberry Jam'

RECIPES FOR A CONTAINER GARDEN

This is the planting list for my container garden that welcomes me in and out of the door every day. I have a collection of around 14 pots, which are moved around and swapped in and out of the main display. I've planted varieties that have hues in orange, pink, red and purple, which makes it an analogous colour scheme (see page 65). I experimented with contrast in the hues, picking some varieties with a lot of shade in their hue, making them appear a rich purple-black, and then played with some of the muddier shades in the heucheras and leaves of the crab apple tree. I love this 'border', and it's fun to add different pops of seasonal colour through the use of tulips and annuals.

See page 98–100 for choosing and preparing containers.

Size: 14 pots of varying sizes.

The largest container in this collection is 60 cm (24 inches) in diameter and 45 cm (18 inches) tall; the smallest is 21 cm (8 inches) in diameter and 18 cm (7 inches) tall.

TALL LAYER (BACK-MIDDLE)

Tree:

- Crab apple *Malus* 'Royalty' x 1 (spring–autumn)

Tall perennials:

- *Sambucus nigra* 'Eva' x 1 (spring–autumn)
- *Actaea* 'Brunette' x 1 (spring–autumn)

MEDIUM LAYER (BACK-MIDDLE)

Medium shrubs:

- *Pittosporum* 'Golf Ball' x 1 (all year round, evergreen)
- Katsura tree x 1 (spring–autumn)
- *Physocarpus* 'Amber Queen' x 2 (spring–autumn)
- *Physocarpus* 'Panther' x 2 (spring–autumn)
- *Spiraea japonica* 'Firelight' x 1 (spring–autumn)

Everything beyond here is tucked in shared pots with larger items.

Medium height perennials:

- *Cirsium rivulare* 'Atropurpureum' x 1 (spring–autumn)
- *Euphorbia* 'Miner's Merlot' x 2 (spring–autumn)

LOW LAYER (MIDDLE-FRONT)

Low-growing perennials:

- *Geranium pratense* 'Midnight Reiter' x 2 (spring–autumn)
- *Heuchera* 'Marmalade' x 2 (all year round)
- *Heuchera* 'Blackberry Jam' x 1 (all year round)
- *Nemesia* 'Wisley Vanilla' x 3 (all year round)
- Creeping thyme x 1

Ground-covering plants:

- Viola 'Rose Blotch' x 5 (autumn–winter, but can be all year round)
- *Viola labradorica* x 3 (autumn–winter, but can be all year round)

Bulbs:

- Snowdrops (winter)
- *Iris reticulata* 'Pauline' (early spring)
- *Crocus* 'Orange Monarch' (early spring)
- Tulip 'Drumline' (later spring)

Annuals:

I swap out the tulips for Cosmos 'Xanthos' (summer–autumn)

HOW TO WORK WITH CONTAINERS

Choose and prepare containers: Select a variety of pots in different sizes with drainage holes. Clean them thoroughly.

Plan your layout: Refer to your planting list to determine the layers – tall plants at the back or centre, medium shrubs and perennials in the middle, and lower-growing plants at the front. Arrange your pots to create a balanced display. Place your container garden in a location that meets the light and temperature needs of your selected varieties.

Add compost: Once your pots are roughly in place, fill with a quality potting mix or seed compost. It's best to have them placed before filling as they can get very heavy and more difficult to move.

Planting: Carefully transplant your plants into each container, ensuring you follow the recommended spacing. If you have a big pot, you might be able to fit in more than one plant. For example, I underplant my potted tree with herbs and small perennials. And I tuck small bulbs and annuals or bedding plants in where there are gaps to create pops of seasonal colour.

Water and position: Water each container thoroughly after planting. Rotate the pots periodically to ensure even sunlight exposure.

Maintenance: Check moisture levels regularly and top up with compost if needed. Refresh your planting by swapping seasonal annuals to keep the display dynamic.

Sambucus nigra 'Eva', *Physocarpus* 'Amber Queen' and *Heuchera* 'Marmalade'

RECIPE FOR A SMALL BORDER

The planting plan here is inspired by a 3.5 x 2 metre (11½ x 6½ feet) space I planted from scratch in autumn 2018. Evergreen shrubs and ferns keep it lush in winter, and the seasons that follow bring interest through bulbs and herbaceous perennials. It's low maintenance, and never fails to lift my spirits.

Size: 3.5 metre (11½ feet) long by 2 m (6½ feet) deep

TALL LAYER (BACK-MIDDLE)

Tree:

- Dwarf crab apple *Malus* 'Aros' x 1 (spring–autumn)

Tall perennials:

- *Filipendula rubra* 'Venusta' (meadowsweet) x 2 (spring–autumn)

MEDIUM LAYER (BACK-MIDDLE)

Medium shrubs:

- *Pittosporum* 'Golf Ball' x 2 (all year round, evergreen)
- Clipped yew ball x 2
- *Hydrangea paniculata* 'Limelight' x 2

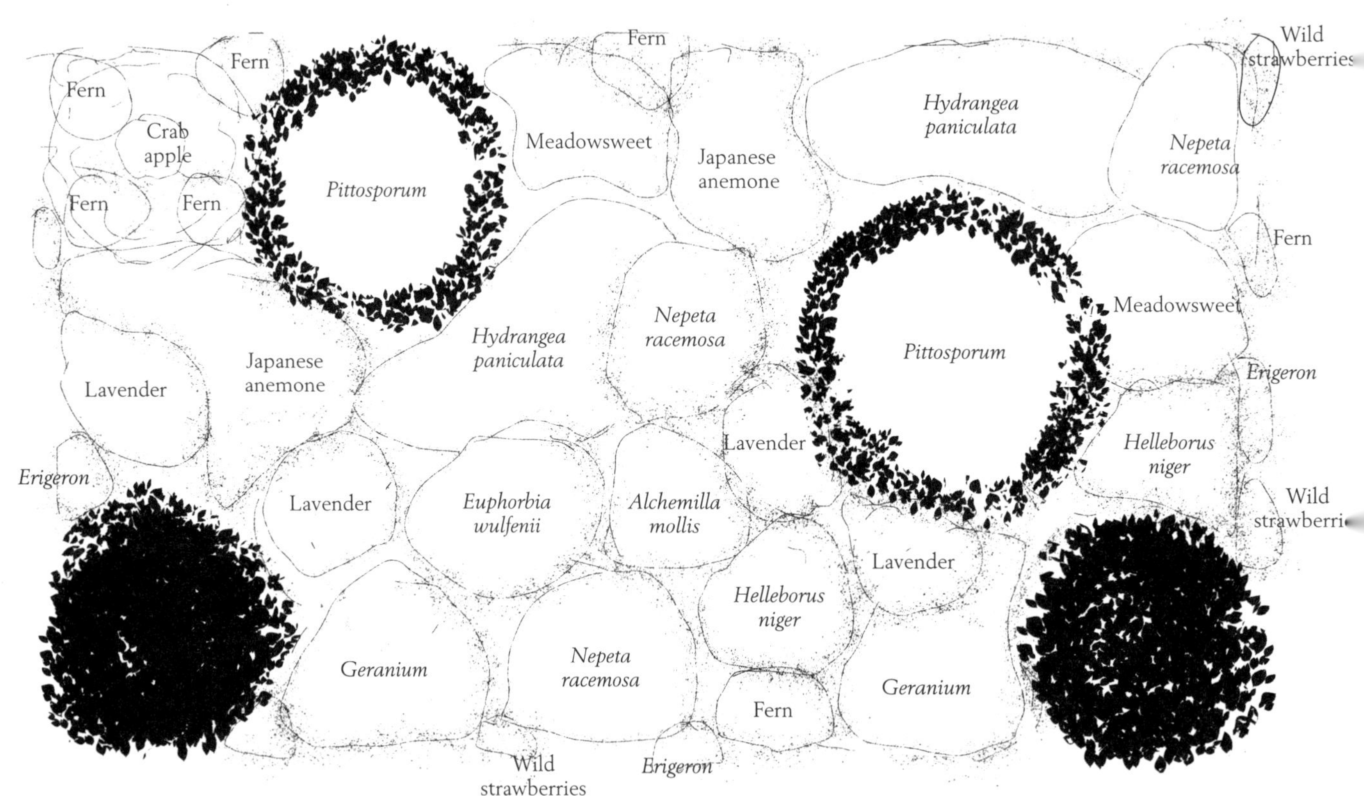

Medium-height perennials:

- *Euphorbia wulfenii* x 1
- Japanese anemone 'Robustissima' x 2 (late-summer–autumn)

LOW LAYER (MIDDLE-FRONT)

Low-growing perennials:

- *Geranium* 'Rozanne Gerwat' x 2 (spring–autumn)
- *Helleborus niger* x 2 (winter–early spring)
- *Nepeta racemosa* 'Walker's Low' x 2
- Lavender x 4

Ground-covering plants:

- *Erigeron karvinskianus* x 4
- Ferns x 7 (all year round)
- *Alchemilla mollis* x 2
- Wild strawberries x 5

Bulbs:

- Snowdrops x 40 (late winter)
- *Crocus chrysanthus* 'Cream Beauty' x 40 (late winter-early spring)
- *Narcissus* 'Moonlight Sensation' x 20 (early spring)
- *Narcissus* 'White Marvel' x 20 (late spring)
- Tulip 'Exotic Emperor' x 20 (mid spring)
- Tulip 'China Town' x 20 (late spring-early summer)

Tall biennial (self-seeders):

- White foxgloves

TALL LAYER (BACK-MIDDLE)

Tree:

- Crab apple *Malus x robusta* 'Red Sentinel' x 1 (spring–autumn)

HOW TO MARK OUT THE BORDER

If creating the border from scratch, outline the dimensions using a garden hose or string. This helps you visualize the space and confirm it's in the ideal location.

PREPARE YOUR BED

Starting from scratch: Lay down cardboard and add compost (see pages 91–2).

Existing border: Clear the area of weeds and debris, then rake the soil and top-dress with compost to improve fertility and drainage.

Place your plants: Divide the border into layers according to your planting plan:

Tall layer: Position the focal tree and tall perennials at the back or centre.

Medium layer: Arrange medium shrubs and perennials next, ensuring they have room to mature.

Low layer: Fill in with low-growing perennials, ground-covering plants and bulbs at the front, then consider adding a few within the middle layer as well.

Place your plants at the suggested spacing to allow for mature growth and to avoid overcrowding. Once planted, step back to assess the overall balance and make any minor adjustments as needed. You can also fill in gaps with annuals or biennials as the border matures.

Planting: Dig appropriate holes for each plant, slightly larger than the root ball of each plant is a good rule. Gently firm the soil around each plant and water thoroughly.

Final touches: Add a layer of mulch to conserve moisture and suppress weeds.

RECIPE FOR A CUTTING GARDEN

The cutting garden has been a generous, giving thread running through my life, a place of inspiration, solace and steady beauty. What began as a small patch of flowers to pick from has, almost a decade as a florist, grew to an acre of blooms on rented farmland. It's supported me through countless weddings, events and long harvest days, and continues to ground my work in rhythm and seasonality.

Along the way, I've come to know which flowers I return to again and again, the ones I love most, the ones that earn their keep by offering armfuls of beauty across the year. I've gathered those favourites into a border-sized plan that works for gardens of all shapes and scales. Every variety included here has been chosen to give generously, with lots of stems from a small space. Some have tall stems for arranging, others are perfect in little bud vases. There's a mix of focal flowers and soft fillers, so everything works together harmoniously. And it's all easy to grow, even if you're just beginning.

If you're carving out a cutting patch of your own, keep your beds no wider than 1 metre (or 3 feet): it makes it easier to reach in and gather flowers as they bloom.

Size: 3 metre (10 feet) long x 1 metre (3 feet) wide

Heuchera 'Marmalade', *Nasturtium* 'Ladybird Rose', Sweet pea 'Castlewellan', *Malope* 'Vulcan' and *Dahlia* 'Jowey Winnie'

FIRST 1-M (3-FOOT) SECTION:

If you interplant dahlias with spring bulbs, you'll get some early spring flowers, and their foliage will be dying back by the time the dahlia foliage starts to put on growth, thus maximizing the season of flowers you can get from the space.

Dahlias: I do think there's a dahlia for every taste, and – these are some of my favourites. Plant 30 cm (12 inches) apart.

- *Dahlia* 'Jowey Winnie' x 2
- *Dahlia* 'Apple Blossom' x 2
- *Dahlia* 'Snowflake' x 2

Spring bulbs: Plant 5–10 cm (2–4 in) apart amongst the dahlias, ensuring they do not touch each other or the dahlia tubers. These bulbs have been chosen for their perennial qualities, if you leave the leaves intact they should continue to come back and flower for you year after year.

- *Leucojum vernum* (early flowering) × 20
- *Muscari* 'Alaska' and 'Early Giant' × 20
- *Narcissus* (early flowering) 'Skype' × 20
- *Narcissus* (late flowering) 'Blushing Lady' × 20
- Tulip (early flowering) 'Mystic Van Eijk' × 20
- Tulip (late flowering) 'China Town' x 20

SECOND 1-M (3-FOOT) SECTION

The annuals listed below are hardworking stalwarts of a cutting garden, and come in a range of disc, spike and umbel forms, giving a perfect mix of flowers for a bouquet.

- *Ammi majus* 'Graceland' × 3
  Plant 30 cm (12 inches) apart.
- Cosmos series 'Cupcakes' × 3
  Plant 30 cm (12 inches) apart.
- *Antirrhinum* 'Appleblossom' × 6
  Plant 22 cm (9 inches) apart.
- *Zinnia* 'Zinderella Lilac' × 6
  Plant 22 cm (9 inches) apart.

THIRD 1-M (3-FOOT) SECTION

I couldn't have a cutting garden without sweet peas. They are the true cut-and-come-again flower – if you cut all the flowers you can see once a week, it will keep the plants flowering for you for months. If you have a hot climate, they will slow down when it gets too hot (consistently above 28–30°C/82–86°F). To mitigate this, you can keep their roots cool by underplanting with compact annuals, and ensure a good cool watering of their roots every day.

Sweet pea pyramid: Plant sweet peas 15 cm (6 inches) apart (see pages 134–5).

- Sweet pea 'Juliet' × 5
- Sweet pea 'Bix' × 5

Underplanted with compact annuals:

- *Viola* 'Peach Shades' × 5
- *Nasturtium* 'Ladybird Rose' × 5

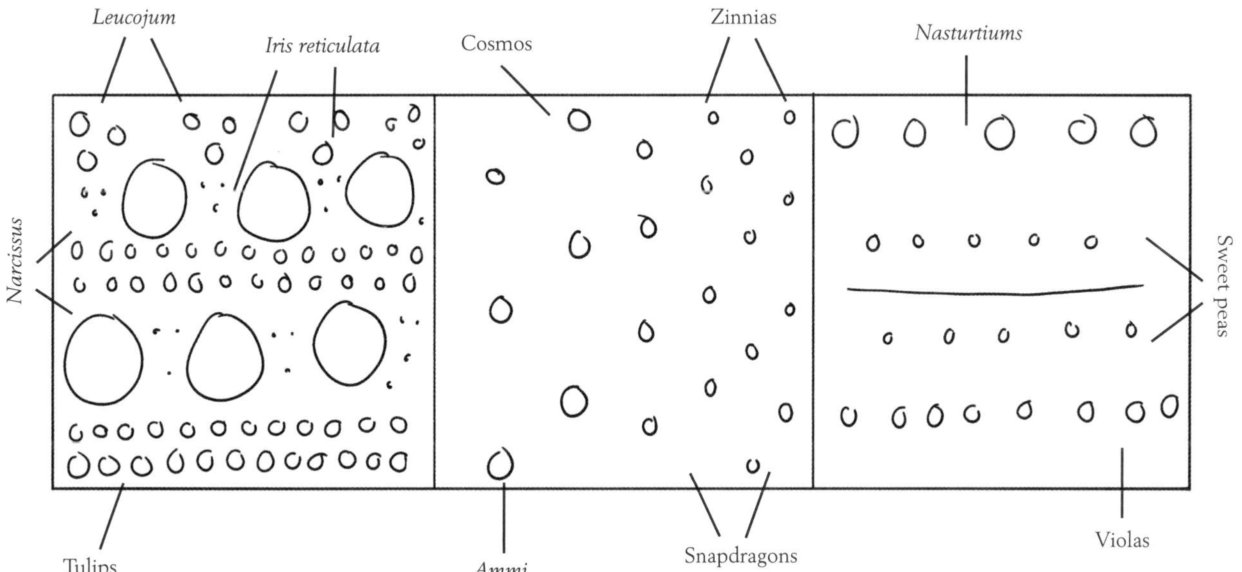

SEASONAL CARE FOR THE CUTTING GARDEN RECIPE

Spring

To Harvest:

- Narcissi and tulips emerge, providing early colour.

To Sow:

- Sow *Nasturtiums*, snapdragons (these can also be sown in autumn), cosmos, violas in early spring, and zinnias once frost is past.
- Pot up your dahlias to start them sprouting.

To Do:

- Perform a weed strike with a hoe.
- Remove any perennial weeds with a trowel or hori-hori.
- Rake the soil in preparation for planting.
- Construct your sweet-pea structure.
- Plant out sweet peas, autumn-sown snapdragons, and Queen Anne's lace (*Ammi majus*).
- In later spring, plant your cosmos, *Nasturtiums*, violas and dahlias.
- If your spring-sown snapdragons are large enough (at least 7.5 cm/3 inches) then plant them out, or wait until early summer.
- Tie in your sweet peas as they grow.

Summer

To Harvest:

- Sweet peas, violas, *Nasturtiums*, cosmos, *Ammi majus* and snapdragons will be followed by dahlias and zinnias.
- Keep picking your flowers – these plants are all cut-and-come-again, meaning they will produce more flowers after those previously picked.

To Sow:

- Sow violas for planting out in autumn to provide winter flowers.
- Sow a second round of zinnias in early summer for successive blooms. When the first zinnia plants slow down, replace them with new seedlings, or remove the *Ammi majus* plants that will be overgrown by late summer, and plant your second succession of zinnias.

To Do:

- Plant out your zinnias and dahlias once all frosts have passed.
- Stake the dahlias now and use twine tied to the stake to support them as they grow.

Autumn

To Harvest:

- Cosmos, *Ammi majus*, snapdragons and zinnias will continue to provide late-season colour until frosts.

To Sow:

- Sow snapdragons, sweet peas and *Ammi majus* now for next year.

To Do:

- Save your seeds.
- Start clearing away plants that have finished flowering.
- Plant your bulbs.

Winter

To Harvest:

- Violas.
- Snowdrops and *Leucojums* will arrive in late winter.

To Sow:

- You can sow sweet peas now for next year if you haven't done so already.

To Do:

- Gently life dahlias and store them over the winter if you are on wet soil and prone to cold winters, as the repeated freeze-thaw cycles can rot dahlia tubers. In places where there is steadier winter weather, try leaving them in the ground and mulch heavily to protect them. In spring, gently remove some of the mulch at their crowns to make sure they're not buried too deep.

Picking Sweet pea 'Windsor'

STRUCTURAL ELEMENTS

STRUCTURAL ELEMENTS

Frameworks that shape space and support growth

Creating a garden doesn't always mean major groundwork or large-scale landscaping. Even small, thoughtful touches can gently shape a space, bringing in balance, intrigue and a sense of welcome. With a few simple ideas, it's possible to design a garden that feels both organized and full of life, without needing heavy machinery or complicated plans.

One of the easiest ways to bring structure into a garden is by using what you already have; plants, fences, walls, gates or arches. If you're working with a larger space, breaking it up into smaller garden 'rooms' (see zoning page 43) can make it feel less overwhelming and more inviting. Much like furnishing a home, dividing up a garden allows you to create moments, corners and calm places to pause. Even smaller spaces can be made to feel larger by diving it into separate 'parts'.

In my own garden, I've used a mix of hedges, fences and even a rough little dry-stone wall I've built over the years. I hesitate to call it that, it's really just a collection of stones I've gathered as I've dug and worked the beds, placed one by one into a low wall. These sorts of boundaries organize the space, and they create a little of that special movement and mystery, drawing the eye forward and offering a sense of discovery, a hint that there's something else to be found just beyond.

What I love about this kind of structure is how adaptable it is. Whether your garden is small or expansive, elements like these help carve out a space that feels personal, cared for and filled with invitations to explore.

Above: *Nasturtium* (*Tropaeolum majus*) 'Climbing Mixed'
Opposite: A hazel pea stick trellis for sweet peas to climb

DIY FENCING

Homemade fences are a versatile addition to any garden. In mine, I use two types: short, knee-height fences and taller ones that reach just below my shoulder. Both are practical and beautiful. They keep curious puppies and toddlers off compost and seedlings, support top-heavy plants against the wind, and break the garden into distinct areas that guide the eye and spark intrigue.

A NOTE ON THE MATERIALS I USE

Stakes: I favour chestnut stakes, at least 10 cm (4 inches) thick. Naturally rot-resistant, chestnut lasts far longer in the ground than most woods without chemical treatment which is ideal in damp climates. The thicker the stake, the longer it lasts, though heavier stakes mean more effort to install. If chestnut isn't available, try oak or cedar, but avoid untreated softwoods, which break down quickly.

Pea sticks: Traditionally used for peas and beans, these flexible, branched stems are also excellent for weaving fences. I use coppiced hazel, which is strong, pliable, and renewable, with plenty of natural side branches that lend a rustic look. If hazel is hard to find, willow (which can root, so take heed) or any long, flexible branches will work, fresh enough to bend without snapping, but sturdy enough to endure the seasons.

FENCING FOR PESKY VISITORS

Living near woodland brings daily wonder; the calls of birds, the shifting light, but also visits from rabbits and deer. Delightful to watch, less so when they feast on the garden.

To deter them, we reinforced the chestnut fence with low chicken wire, buried slightly to stop rabbits burrowing through. For deer, we added two simple wires above the fence: barely visible, but Enough to break their line of sight and nudge them elsewhere. Rabbits and deer usually follow the path of least resistance, and now they wander around rather than through. This method keeps the garden protected while staying soft on the landscape. If deer persist, a taller, more robust fence may be needed.

TIP

If you don't have access to hazel, other materials like willow or any long, flexible branches can be used as alternatives. Just make sure they're fresh enough to bend without snapping but sturdy enough to last through the seasons.

HOW TO MAKE A SHORT FENCE

Short fencing is a simple, effective way to add structure to a garden, guiding the eye and gently dividing space without closing it off. There is a narrow strip of unused lawn between the house and back gate that was ideal to plant my peony crop. I wanted to make the beds into planted corridors, something beautiful to walk through, not just past. By laying out beds and adding low fencing made from chestnut stakes, a transitional space was turned into a destination in its own right. This kind of fencing is easy to make, endlessly adaptable, and offers support for plants (especially handy for top-heavy peonies in full flower), boundaries for children and pets, and a strong visual framework for your garden 'rooms'.

You will need:

- **Chestnut stakes:** Around 4 cm (1½ inches) thick and knee height (about 45–50 cm/18–20 inches)
- **String (optional):** To help ensure alignment
- **Drill:** For creating holes in the stakes
- **Copper wire:** Flexible but strong enough to hold the structure together
- **Mallet:** For driving stakes into the ground
- **Pea sticks:** Straight, sturdy and pliable branches for the cross-supports

1. PLAN YOUR FENCE LINE
Decide where your short fence will go and mark the line. Use string stretched between two stakes as a guide to keep the fence straight.

2. PREPARE THE STAKES
Drill a hole through the top of each chestnut stake, approximately 2.5–5 cm (1–2 inches) from the top. The holes should be wide enough to thread your copper wire through.

3. INSTALL THE STAKES
Position a stake every 1–1.5 metre (3–5 feet) along the fence line. Use a mallet to drive each stake firmly into the ground, ensuring they are straight and stable. The stakes should be deep enough to withstand pressure from the wire and pea sticks (10–15 cm/ 4–6 inches is a good depth).

4. THREAD THE COPPER WIRE
Starting at one end of the fence, thread the copper wire through the drilled holes in the stakes. Keep the wire taut as you go to ensure the fence is sturdy.

5. ATTACH THE PEA STICKS

Once the wire is in place, hold up a pea stick between each pair of stakes. Secure the pea sticks to the wire by twisting the copper wire tightly around them, ensuring they are held firmly in place. The pea sticks should run horizontally, providing a natural, rustic aesthetic, as well offering ample support to the plants grown beside them.

6. TEST FOR STABILITY

Gently push on the fence to ensure it is stable. Adjust the wire or stakes as needed to tighten the structure.

Rose 'Kew Gardens' and *Ammi majus (Queen Anne's lace)*

HOW TO MAKE A TALL FENCE

The taller woven fences I make for the garden add both structure and softness to the space. They're functional, offering protection from wind, marking boundaries, and supporting climbers, but they also bring a beautiful, handmade texture that blends naturally into the landscape. This style of fencing is slightly more involved than the shorter version, but still very achievable with a bit of planning, some sturdy stakes (and a willing helper).

You will need:

- **Sturdy stakes:** These form the backbone of your fence. You can choose the height you require. Remember, a good portion will need to be under the ground for the fence to be secure.
- **Pea sticks:** Flexible branches for weaving between the stakes
- **String (optional):** To help ensure alignment
- **Spade:** To dig holes
- **Mallet or post rammer:** For driving stakes deep into the ground
- **Friend (optional but helpful):** Extra hands make the weaving process easier

Sweet pea 'Blush'

1. PLAN YOUR FENCE

Decide where the fence will go and space your stakes about 60 cm (2 feet) apart (you can adjust the spacing based on the desired appearance). Stretch a length of string between two stakes as a guide to keep the fence straight. Lay a pea stick or similar guide on the ground to help with spacing, you want to ensure the pea sticks can be woven through multiple stakes for added tension and stability.

2. INSTALL THE STAKES

Dig a deep hole (approximately one third of the stake's height) for each stake to ensure stability. Insert the first stake into the hole and use a mallet or post rammer to drive it securely into the ground.

3. BACKFILL THE HOLE

Pack the soil tightly, stamping the compost in with your foot to limit movement. Repeat with the remaining stakes.

4. WEAVE THE PEA STICKS

Start at the bottom of the stakes, weaving pea sticks or flexible branches horizontally through the stakes. Work your way up, maintaining even tension for a strong and visually appealing result. A friend can hold the stakes steady and help with tension during weaving for a cleaner finish.

HOW TO MAKE AN ARCH

An arch is perfect for training climbing plants such as roses, clematis or sweet peas, adding height and charm to your garden.

You will need:

- **Spade:** To dig holes
- **Heavy-duty stakes:** At least four, sturdy enough to support the structure
- **Mallet or post rammer:** For driving stakes deep into the ground
- **Pea sticks:** Flexible yet durable for reinforcing and shaping
- **Bendable stems:** Such as willow or hazel for the top curve
- **Twine, string or wire:** For securely lashing the structure together
- **A friend (optional but helpful):** Working in a pair helps to makes the lashing and reinforcement process easier

1. INSTALL THE UPRIGHT STAKES

Decide on the arch's location and mark the spots where the stakes will be placed. Choose heavy-duty stakes approximately 1.8–2.4 metre (6–8 feet) long. For optimal stability, plan to bury about one-quarter to one-third of each stake's height underground. Dig deep holes at the marked locations. The depth should be sufficient to accommodate the required portion of each stake below ground. Place each stake in its hole and use a mallet or a post rammer to drive the stakes down firmly, ensuring they reach the necessary depth. Backfill the holes with the excavated soil and tightly pack it down to secure each stake firmly in place.

2. REINFORCE THE STAKES

I use hazel pea sticks to reinforce the stakes by lashing them horizontally between the uprights. Secure them tightly with twine, string or wire to ensure the structure is stable. Add horizontal reinforcements at multiple levels to create a robust framework. Work your way up, as it's always easier to start from the lower points.

3. CREATE THE TOP CURVE

Select flexible materials, such as willow or hazel pea sticks, for the arch's curve. Twist the stems around each other to add strength and create a sturdy, cohesive curve. Attach the curve by lashing the twisted stems securely to the tops of the stakes, ensuring even tension and alignment.

4. MAINTAIN YOUR ARCH

While the heavy-duty stakes can last for years, the pea sticks and willow stems may need replacing annually or as they wear out. Regularly check the arch for stability, and reinforce as needed to ensure it remains functional and safe for climbing plants.

PLANT SUPPORTS

HOW TO SUPPORT TALL PLANTS

Tall plants often struggle to stay upright, and while nature usually lets them recover just enough to lift their flowers above the grasses for pollination, our gardens require a bit more order. Tall species are typically planted at the back of borders to showcase their height, but without support, they can end up in a tangled mess, falling onto their neighbours. This is where staking comes to the rescue.

Using stakes and twine is a simply and fairly quick and easy way to deal with taller plants before they grow to a height where toppling might occur. With the right support, plants can thrive without falling sideways, and the whole space can feel more generous, more layered, and more at ease.

THE CHALLENGES OF STAKING

Staking can feel like a frustrating chore. Twine has a knack of tangling at the worst moments, scissors always seem to vanish, and there's inevitably a large, immovable stone exactly where you want to place a stake. Despite these challenges, staking is well worth the effort, especially if you have witnessed a storm wreak havoc on tall plants in a single night. Without support, many plants simply collapse and end up needing drastic pruning just as they hit their peak flowering moment.

AN ALTERNATIVE: THE CHELSEA CHOP

If staking isn't your thing, you can try cutting plants back before midsummer. This technique, known in the UK as the 'Chelsea Chop' (timed to coincide with the RHS Chelsea Flower Show in May), works particularly well for clump-forming plants, such as phlox and *Hylotelephium*. By cutting them back early, you'll encourage bushier, more compact growth that's less likely to flop. While this method delays flowering, it also reduces the need for staking and produces sturdier plants.

EMERGENCY STAKING FOR FALLEN PLANTS

We all have moments where staking gets forgotten or overlooked. Sometimes, a plant you didn't think needed staking ends up sprawled across its neighbours. In these cases:

Give it time: Wait a day or two to see if the plant can lift itself up naturally.

Minimal support: Use a single stake and some twine to gently tie it back into position.

Cut it back: If it's too tangled or damaged to recover, trim it back and let it regrow.

PREVENTATIVE STAKING

The best time to stake plants is before they start to fall over. If you can stake in spring, you'll save yourself time and frustration later. My preferred stakes are chestnut or hazel pea sticks. Here's a simple technique:

Shape: Create a pyramid of stakes around the plant, with the point of the pyramid at about two-thirds of the plant's expected height. Where the stakes meet, lash the tops with twine, ensuring that they're tied securely.

Grow through: As the plant grows, it will fill out and hide the stakes, giving the support a natural and unobtrusive look.

By summer, you won't even notice the stakes, and the plant will look beautifully upright and layered. You don't need to be too neat about it – just ensure the stakes are sturdy and the twine is secure.

KEEP IT SIMPLE

For now, my staking is practical rather than ornamental – just sticks and twine, and that works perfectly well. One day, I'd love to spend more time crafting elegant, decorative plant supports, but for now, functionality is what matters. After all, the goal is to let the plants shine, and with very little effort in the spring, you'll have a garden full of towering, thriving blooms that will remain supported no matter what the weather brings.

CORRALLING

For plants grown in clusters, one method I love is corralling (see above). I set short stakes at regular intervals around the plants and criss-cross twine between them to create a supportive grid that guides and stabilizes growth, making sure that the twine is taut and tied tightly. Corralling is particularly useful for plants that are naturally sprawling, climbing or prone to falling over. In windy or rainy conditions, the support from the twine helps the plants maintain their shape and stay upright.

Honesty amidst Sweet pea 'Alisa' having an 'emergency single stake' treatment after falling

STRUCTURES FOR CLIMBING PLANTS

Sweet peas are one of my favourite plants to grow in the garden, as not only are they beautiful, colourful and scented, they're also so easy to grow, are very rewarding and the more you cut for your home, the more they flower. I couldn't be without them, so every year I make plenty of structures around the garden for them to climb. Creating sturdy and attractive structures for climbing plants is a way to add height, interest, and functionality to your space. And it doesn't just have to be sweet peas, there are plenty of annual climbers (*Cobaea scandens*, climbing *Nasturtiums*, and beans to name a few) that look wonderful on these types of supports. Here are two simple designs I often use for climbing plants: a trellis-style support and a freestanding pyramid.

TIPS FOR BOTH DESIGNS

Strength and stability: Always ensure your poles or sticks are deeply secured in the soil. Packing the soil tightly around the base of each pole is crucial for stability.

Twine: Use a durable twine for lashing and netting to prevent wear over time.

Plant placement: I generally plant the seedlings out close to where the poles are, but as long as you have netting, twine or short support branches for them to grab, plant them at their recommended spacing (for sweet peas try 20 cm (8 in) apart). Train the climbing plants gently towards the structure as they grow, helping them find the supports and start climbing.

Seasonal maintenance: Replace worn twine and damaged poles at the start of each growing season. The thickness of the poles determines if they can be used for more than one season or not. The thicker they are, the longer they'll last.

TRELLIS-STYLE SUPPORT

This design works beautifully for longer runs of climbing plants, such as sweet peas, beans or cobaea. It's simple to construct and incredibly sturdy when done right.

1. CHOOSE YOUR POLES
Use tall, thick bean poles or sturdy branches. The length of the poles will depend on how tall you want the trellis, but I find 2.5–3 metre (8–10 feet) works well for most climbing plants. Ensure at least 60 cm (2 feet) of each pole is pushed firmly into the ground.

2. POSITION THE POLES
Place two poles opposite each other, roughly 30 cm (12 inches) apart. Repeat this pairing every 90 cm (3 feet) along the length of your desired trellis. If your soil is particularly hard or the poles are very thick, you may need to dig small holes to secure the base of each pole. Angle the poles towards each other to create the V shape for the crossbar to nestle in. Once in place, pack the soil tightly around the poles to ensure stability.

3. ADD THE CROSSBAR
Lay a horizontal bean pole across the top, aligning it with where the pairs meet. Lash it securely to the vertical poles using strong twine or jute.

4. TIE IN

Wrap the twine tightly around the joints several times, ensuring the crossbar is sturdy enough to support the climbing plants.

5. ADD NETTING

Hang twine or a simple net from the horizontal crossbar, letting it drape down to the soil. Tension is important to give the most support for the plants as they climb. If you're using just single strands of twine, bury them in the ground to give them some tension. With a net, make sure it's taut.

PYRAMID-STYLE SUPPORT

A freestanding pyramid structure is ideal for smaller spaces and individual climbing plants. It's another great choice for annual climbers, such as sweet peas and *Nasturtiums*, offering both functionality and charm.

1. SELECT YOUR PEA STICKS

Choose 5–6 sturdy, straight pea sticks or thin poles. They should be at least 1.5–1.8 metre (5–6 feet) long for a well-proportioned pyramid.

2. FORM THE BASE

Push the sticks into the ground in a circular pattern, ensuring even spacing between each. A diameter of about 60–90 cm (2–3 feet) works well. Make sure each stick is buried securely, about 15–30 cm (6–12 inches) into the soil, depending on its thickness and your soil type.

3. BIND THE TOP

Pull the tops of the sticks together to form a pyramid shape. Lash them securely with twine, wrapping it multiple times and tying a strong knot to ensure the structure stays in place.

4. ADD EXTRA BRANCH SUPPORT

I twist pliable willow stems together and weave them around the pyramid structures. I also collect shorter, fan-shaped branches to create additional horizontal supports. Push these branches into the ground between the pea sticks and weave them around the pyramid frame. These will act as extra support for plants to grab onto as they climb.

MAKING A PATH

Paths act as part of the bones of a garden; strong lines that hold the space together. Even in the depths of winter, when planting has died back, a well-designed path can carry the eye and keep the garden looking beautiful and intentional. Once you've decided whether you want straight, curved or meandering paths (see page 47), and what material you want to use (see page 50), you can mark them out in the space, ready to lay.

You will need:

- **Garden hose or string:** To serve as a flexible guide
- **Stakes:** To secure the string or hose
- **Non-permanent marking paint or spray paint:** To clearly define the path boundaries
- **Spade, hoe or rake (or a manual excavator for large areas):** To prepare the ground
- **Base layer:** See step 3
- **Path materials of your choice:** See step 4

1. MARK THE ROUTE OF THE PATH

Lay a garden hose or length of string along the desired path route to serve as a flexible guide. For more precise marking, place stakes at regular intervals and secure the hose or string to them. Walk along the marked path to ensure it flows naturally, and adjust the hose or string as necessary. For curved paths, gently bend the hose or string to achieve a smooth, flowing line without sharp angles.

2. PREPARING AND EXCAVATING THE PATHWAY

Use a shovel or garden hoe to remove grass, weeds and other vegetation within the marked path. You will need to excavate to an appropriate depth, depending on the material you are using for your path. If using wood chips, you can lay cardboard and spread the chips on top without the need for excavating further.

Depth requirements:

Gravel or crushed stone: 10–15 cm (4–6 inches)

Pavers or bricks: 15–20 cm (6–8 inches)

Natural stone or flagstone: 15–20 cm (6–8 inches)

Ensure a flat, level base by using a rake to smooth the excavated soil, removing any large clumps or debris. Walk along the path to ensure it's flat and even, making adjustments as necessary.

3. ADDING A BASE MATERIAL

The base layer provides a stable foundation that prevents the path surface from shifting, sinking or becoming uneven over time, especially in areas with varying soil conditions. It can help with drainage and control weed growth. Slightly slope the base away from structures (e.g. your home) to help the water move in a different direction.

Gravel or crushed stone paths: Add a 5–7.5-cm (2–3-inch) base layer of compacted gravel or crushed stone. Use a tamper or plate compactor to firmly compact the base material, minimizing future shifting.

Pavers or stone paths: Lay a 10–15-cm (4–6-inch) base layer of crushed stone or sand. Spread the material evenly and compact it thoroughly to create a solid foundation.

4. LAYING THE PATH

For gravel or crushed stone paths: Evenly spread the material, using a rake to distribute gravel or mulch uniformly over the prepared base. Create a consistent surface by ensuring the material covers the entire path area without gaps or uneven patches.

For stone pavers, flagstones and bricks: Start from a corner or edge, laying pavers or bricks from a fixed point. Use spacers or a pattern guide to keep gaps between pavers or bricks uniform. Leave small gaps (optional) between stones to allow grass, moss, or low-growing plants, such as creeping thyme or chamomile, to fill them, enhancing the natural look. Use a rubber mallet to gently tap each paver or brick into position, ensuring it sits firmly on the base.

MAKING A PLACE TO SIT

When you love to garden, it's easy to forget sometimes that a garden is also a place to live, unwind and enjoy, not just tend to. Creating a seating area in your garden transforms it from a place of seasonal chores into an extension of your home. It invites you to slow down, to savour the space you've cultivated and to experience it in a whole new way. Whether it's a corner for a morning coffee or a spot to gather with loved ones, no matter how simple, a garden seat can bring joy to your daily life.

If there's room, I will always recommend having more than one seating area. Even small gardens can usually accommodate two little spots. Perhaps one could be a cozy nook for a quick cup of tea or a glass of wine, while the other spot might have a little table set up for meals or gathering with friends. Think about the sun and shade at different times of day; where's the perfect place to catch the morning light or to retreat from the midday heat?

In my garden, I have a favourite place just by the back door. It catches the early light, and so it's where I take my tea on warm mornings. In the evenings, it becomes a calm, quiet place that overlooks the cutting patch where I can sit and still hear my son if he stirs. These little moments in the garden each day have bound the outdoor space into the rhythm of my daily life in such a lovely way.

I like to find second-hand furniture for these spaces. Metal pieces age well outdoors, and I make them softer with cushions and blankets. A little vase of flowers helps too, even just a few stems. It's worth keeping cushions dry, bringing them in overnight or storing them in a box or bench.

A seating area doesn't need to be elaborate or costly to feel special. A simple bench tucked beneath a tree or a folding chair placed in a sunny corner can create a space that feels like an extension of your living room. It's all about making your garden a place you want to linger in, not just work on. A place to rest, connect, and feel a little more grounded.

Rose 'Kathleen Harrop', now hard to find, but 'Generous Gardener' is a lovely alternative

WATER IN THE GARDEN

Water is one of the most important ways to support wildlife in the garden. Birds, insects, amphibians and even small mammals rely on it, for drinking, bathing, breeding, or just somewhere cool to rest. You don't need a big pond to make a difference. Even a small container of water can become a haven.

If you're lucky with your pond, you'll soon enjoy the buzz of dragonflies, and the splashes of frogs, and sometimes the sight of birds dipping in for a drink. One of my favourite things about our container pond is how much my toddler loves it. He dips his little cup into the water again and again, determined to 'help' water the plants. His curiosity, his persistence, it's unexpectedly effective, and endlessly sweet, and now he's actually quite helpful!

CREATING A CONTAINER POND

The best time to build a container pond is in spring or early summer, as plants establish quickly and wildlife is most active.

You will need:

- **Recycled container:** You can think as creatively as you like; reclaimed sinks, half-barrels or large tubs all work beautifully; check it is watertight
- **Stones, bricks or logs:** To create ramps and shelter for wildlife
- **Compact pond plants:** Choose plants that thrive in small water features (see page 141)
- **Rainwater:** Use water from a water butt

Hydrangea 'Limelight', *Erigeron*, *Pittosporum* 'Golf Ball' *Geranium* 'Rozanne', Deer fern and *Euphorbia wulfenii*

Geranium 'Rozanne' and Hydrangea 'Limelight' in The Well Garden border (see page 106 for planting plan).

1. CHOOSE THE LOCATION
Pick a spot where you can easily view and enjoy the pond. A mix of sun and shade is ideal, as too much sun can warm the water excessively. Position it safely if you have young children – a simple barrier or thoughtful placement is all that's needed.

2. FILL WITH RAINWATER
Use rainwater from a water butt, as tap water can introduce excess nutrients, leading to algae growth.

3. MAKE IT WILDLIFE-FRIENDLY
Add ramps, such as stacks of stones, bricks, or a plank of untreated wood covered with chicken wire, as it's important for wildlife to be able to get in and out of the container with ease. Surround the pond with rocks, pots or plants to provide shelter and hiding spots for creatures.

4. ADD POND PLANTS

Choose a mix of floating and upright plants to provide shelter and oxygenate the water. Compact species, such as my favourite *Nymphaea* 'Pygmaea Rubra' (mini waterlily), are perfect for small ponds. Gently lower your plants into the water, ensuring they are spaced to allow for growth.

5. LET NATURE TAKE OVER

Be patient and allow wildlife to find the pond naturally. Avoid transferring pond water, frogspawn or creatures from other sources to prevent introducing diseases or invasive species.

CARING FOR YOUR POND

Top up water: Check the water level regularly, especially in hot weather, and top up with rainwater as needed.

Control algae and debris: Scoop out excess pondweed or algae, and remove any dead leaves to keep the water clear and healthy.

Add oxygen: Consider a solar-powered fountain or bubble aerator to oxygenate the water and keep it fresh. This will also help to prevent mosquitoes from breeding in it.

Trim plants: Remove fading or dead plant material to prevent it from decaying in the water.

MY FAVOURITE PLANTS FOR A CONTAINER POND

Floating: Mini waterlily, frogbit, water soldier

Oxygenating: Hornwort, water crow-foot

Marginal: Water iris, marsh marigold, water forget-me-not, giant cowslip

Low-growing: Brooklime, creeping Jenny

A NOTE ON DUCKWEED

Duckweed is a floating plant that can spread rapidly, which gives it a reputation for being a nuisance. However, it can be excellent for providing shelter for newts, tadpoles, common frogs and common toads. It is also high in protein, so a beneficial food source for ducks, fish and tadpoles. I've added some to my small container pond, as it will help prevent water evaporation on hot days, and also help to keep down breeding mosquitoes. You might not want to introduce it to a larger pond, but you can simply manage it by gently sweeping it out regularly with a net (this will help the pond to retain a balanced ecosystem and allow some light to reach plants lower in the pond).

A NOTE ON GIANT COWSLIP

Giant Cowslip (pictured left) copes well with wet conditions, ensure it sits on a rock or on the edge of your pond with the crown and leaves above the water line.

ESSENTIAL SKILLS

PROPAGATION FROM SEED

The cost of buying plants can add up quickly when you're creating a garden, so by having a few simple propagation tricks up your sleeve, a lot more possibilities become available, Suddenly, expanding your garden becomes almost free, and there's something so satisfying about multiplying your favourite plants yourself. Whether it's taking cuttings, dividing perennials or saving seeds, these skills can make all the difference.

Growing from seed is my favourite way to grow and raise thousands of plants every year for the garden. You don't need much space or special equipment. You can collect seed from plants or buy a packet of a particular variety at a reasonable cost, with each packet providing the opportunity to propagate many, many plants.

If you go on to collect the seeds from the plant you grow each year, the seed will introduce new genetics with each generation, so you may notice subtle changes or delightful variations year after year.

There are two main times of year when I sow seeds: autumn and spring. In autumn, I sow hardy annuals, these are plants that can tolerate colder temperatures and keep growing slowly through the winter. Some even need the cold to kick-start germination, a process called cold stratification or vernalisation. Spring, on the other hand, is when we sow more tender annuals that prefer warmer soil and milder conditions to get going.

There are also two main ways to sow seeds: directly into the soil, or into trays and pots. Each method has its benefits, and in this section I'll walk you through both. Which one you choose can depend on your space, climate, and the kind of seeds you're working with.

Each seed variety will have slightly different needs; some need light to germinate, others prefer darkness; some like warmth, others will happily germinate in cooler conditions. Your seed packet should guide you on the specific requirements, so have a read before you begin.

DIRECT SOWING

Direct sowing is a simple and satisfying way to start your garden. By planting seeds straight into the ground, you save time and give plants a chance to establish themselves exactly where they'll grow.

You will need:

- **Rake:** To level the soil and break it into a fine, crumbly texture
- **Seeds:** Your chosen annuals, biennials or perennials that thrive when sown directly into the ground. Check the seed packet for sowing instructions specific to each type
- **Watering can or hose with gentle spray attachment:** To provide consistent moisture without disturbing the seeds. A fine spray prevents seeds from being washed away
- **Hoe or trowel (optional):** Useful for creating furrows or shallow holes at the correct depth for larger seeds
- **Frost cloth or mini polytunnel materials (optional)**: Wire hoops and frost cloth (also known as fleece)can help protect seedlings from unexpected cold snaps
- **Mulch (optional):** A thin layer of mulch (see page 200) laid and raked into the border before sowing can help retain moisture and prevent weed growth

WHEN TO SOW DIRECTLY

Spring: The best time to direct sow is when the soil has warmed up and the risk of frost has passed. For hardy annuals, you can sow earlier (late March to April), but tender plants should wait until late spring (May).

Autumn: Hardy annuals, such as cornflowers, larkspur and nigella, can be sown in autumn. They will overwinter and bloom earlier the following year.

Before sowing, check your local weather forecast and soil conditions. The soil should be workable (i.e. not too wet or frozen) and heavy rain should not be expected within a day or two of sowing.

TIPS

Plan for succession planting: You can sow small batches of annuals every few weeks and they should flower at intervals to extend the flowering season for you.

Mulch lightly: Once seedlings are established and are at least 5–7.5 cm (2–3 inches) tall, a thin layer of mulch can help retain soil moisture and reduce weeds.

Be patient: Germination times vary, so don't worry if some seeds take longer to sprout.

NOTE

Hardy annuals can tolerate cold down to about -10°C (14°F), or sometimes even to -15°C (5°F) if their roots are well established.

1. CHOOSE THE RIGHT LOCATION
Select a sunny spot where your annuals will receive at least 6–8 hours of sunlight a day. Ensure the soil is well-draining and fertile.

2. PREPARE THE BED
Remove any weeds or debris. Rake the soil to a fine tilth – this is a crumbly, lump-free surface that's easy for tiny seeds and roots to navigate.

3. SOW AT THE RIGHT DEPTH
Most seeds should be sown at a depth equal to twice their size. Check the seed packet for specific instructions on depth and spacing.

4. WATERING
Keep the soil moist but not waterlogged. Water regularly to ensure consistent moisture, but avoid overwatering as it can lead to rot or risk washing the seeds away. Try to sow when no heavy rain is forecast to prevent seeds from washing away.

5. THIN SEEDLINGS
Once seedlings have germinated, thin them out by removing smaller or weaker ones. This gives each plant enough space to grow and prevents crowding.

6. PROTECT SEEDLINGS
Watch for less welcome creatures and diseases, and take action as needed. Use nematodes for slugs and fine mesh to protect from other creatures. If a sudden cold snap is forecast, create a mini polytunnel using wire hoops and frost cloth to protect seedlings.

SOWING IN SEED TRAYS, CELLS AND POTS

Sowing seeds in trays is a fantastic way to give your plants the best possible start in a controlled environment. Whether you're using a greenhouse, a cold frame or a sunny windowsill, or even a table out in the elements, this method allows you to carefully monitor germination and early growth. (See page 19 for seed starting tool kit).

A GUIDE TO SEED TRAYS

Seed trays provide a convenient, organized way to start seeds and nurture healthy seedlings for your garden. My business partner, Paris, and I have spent years sourcing and trialing seed trays as we've expanded our flower business and these are our learnings from along the way.

Consistency: By starting seeds in a single tray, you can manage all your seedlings at once, ensuring they receive the same care. Watering, feeding and moving them around becomes much easier when everything is contained in one place.

Convenience: When it's time to transplant your seedlings, having them all in one tray simplifies the process, as you can easily transport the entire tray to your planting site.

Standard design: Most seed trays are designed with a standard length and width to fit into bottom-watering trays (my preferred way to water most of my seedlings). They come in standardized ¼, ½ and full sizes. This makes them compatible with a variety of gardening set-ups, from greenhouses to home windowsills.

Trays or cell trays: We have settled on using trays without cells for smaller seeds like nicotiana, or varieties with erratic germination like larkspur, we then prick out the seedling into cell trays. We prefer using cell trays from the start for seeds that are larger and quicker to germinate seeds like cosmos.

A GUIDE TO CELL TRAYS

One of the main differences between seed trays is the number of cells they contain, which directly affects the size of each individual cell. Larger trays with fewer cells require more space in the greenhouse but they allow seedlings to grow bigger before transplanting, which can eliminate the extra job of potting on. Trays typically come in a range of configurations, such as:

Fewer cells (e.g. 32, 50): Large cells provide space for seedlings to develop their roots and top growth.

More cells (e.g. 72, 128, 288): Small cells are better for starting many seeds at once but offer less room for root development.

We have found that a 7 x 11 cells seed tray is ideal for mass propagating most of our seedlings. Each cell is approximately 4 cm (1¾ inches) wide and 5 cm (2 inches) deep, providing the perfect environment for a variety of plants

GUIDELINES FOR DIFFERENT PLANT TYPES

Large-rooted plants: These plants benefit from large cells to accommodate their rapid growth and extensive root systems. The extra space ensures they develop strong, healthy roots without becoming overcrowded. **Examples:** cerinthe, sunflower

Smaller or slower-growing plants: These plants can thrive in trays with more cells than our standard 7 x 11 cell tray, save space in your propagation zone by giving them smaller cells. **Examples:** lettuce, rudbeckia.

Sweet peas: We sow 2–3 seeds per cell in 9-cm (3½-inch) pots. This approach allows each sweet pea seedling enough room to grow robustly, ensuring better germination rates and healthier plants.

MY SEED POTTING MIX RECIPE

At the flower farm, we have trialled so many seed composts. I find that many off-the-rack bags of seed or potting compost dry out quickly or are too dense, so I have developed my own mixture that does a good job for everything I grow. Measure 6 parts coir fibre, 6 parts sifted compost, 1 part perlite and 1 part vermiculite and mix together well. For a simpler version try 6 parts multipurpose compost with 1 part horticultural grit or perlite.

ASTER

FIRST CHOOSE YOUR TRAY

You will need:

- **Cell trays or standard trays:** Choose a size based on your seeds and available space. Trays with individual module cells are great for individual plants, while standard trays suit smaller seeds that you can scatter and then prick out into individual cells or pots once they've germinated. You can also use pots for sowing straight into, I like a 9-cm (4-inch) pots for larger seedlings like sunflowers and sweet peas.
- **Multipurpose compost:** Use high-quality compost to provide essential nutrients for germination, or the seed compost recipe on page 148.
- **Horticultural grit or perlite (optional):** Improves drainage and creates a lighter, more oxygen-rich compost mix for seedling roots.
- **Watering can with fine rose, or spray bottle:** Ensures gentle watering without displacing seeds.
- **Propagation lid (optional):** Helps retain moisture and creates a humid environment for germination; can also protect seeds from being eaten by rodents while they germinate.
- **Dibber or pencil (optional):** Useful for pressing seeds into the compost, or pricking out seedlings later.
- **Tray for bottom watering:** A shallow tray holding water that is placed under a seed tray for bottom watering; this reduces disturbance to seeds.

1. PREPARE THE POTTING COMPOST / POTTING MIX

If not using a pre-made seed potting mix then mix your compost using the seed potting mix recipe on page 148. Fill your trays or modules with the compost mixture, lightly firming it down without compacting.

2. REMOVE AIR POCKETS

Tap the tray gently on your work surface to remove any large air pockets that could dry out seedlings. Top up any sunken cells with more compost.

3. WATER BEFORE SOWING

Water the trays or modules thoroughly so the compost is moist but not soggy. Pre-moistening ensures seeds won't move around when you water later.

4. SOW THE SEEDS

In standard trays: Sow seeds thinly and evenly across the surface of the compost.

In cell/module trays or pots: Place 1–2 seeds in the centre of each cell. Press the seeds gently into the compost with your finger or a dibber.

5. COVER THE SEEDS

Cover the seeds with a thin layer of compost or vermiculite (a lightweight mineral that retains water and keeps soil airy, helping seeds stay moist for germination), about the same depth as the size of the seed. If the seeds require light to germinate (check the seed packet), omit the compost layer and instead use a propagation lid (see page 150) or clingfilm to retain moisture.

6. WATER FROM BELOW

Place the trays or modules in a shallow tray of water, allowing the compost to soak up moisture from the bottom. This prevents the seeds from being displaced. Remove once the surface feels damp.

7. PROVIDE THE RIGHT ENVIRONMENT`

Temperature: Hardy annuals do well in an unheated greenhouse or outdoors. Tender plants may need warmth, such as a heated greenhouse or indoors on a sunny windowsill.

Ventilation: Ensure good airflow to prevent diseases, such as damping off, indicated by spindly stems.

Light: If using a windowsill, move seedlings outdoors once germinated to prevent weak, leggy growth.

8. MAINTAIN MOISTURE

Keep the compost consistently moist but not waterlogged. Use a fine spray or bottom watering to maintain even moisture levels.

9. PRICK OUT AND TRANSPLANT

(See page 154 for more details) Once the seedlings have developed their first true leaves and are large enough to handle, carefully prick them out with a dibber or pencil. Transplant them into individual pots or directly into the garden, giving them enough space to grow.

TIPS

Timing: Start sowing hardy annuals in late winter to early spring, or in autumn for overwintering. Tender plants should be sown in late spring after the risk of frost has passed.

Don't overheat: Avoid keeping seedlings too warm for too long. Excess warmth signals them to grow top-heavy at the expense of root development, which weakens the plants in the long term.

Label your seeds: It's easy to forget which seeds you've sown, so label trays clearly with plant names and dates (see page 19).

Air flow: If growing in a greenhouse or tunnel, be sure to open the doors and windows every day if the weather allows. Good air circulation helps to prevent the build-up of disease.

A note on starting seeds in the home: If you're starting seeds indoors at home, it's worth noting that even a bright windowsill may not provide enough light for healthy seedlings. Indoor temperatures are often too warm, which can encourage weak, leggy growth as seedlings focus on reaching for light instead of developing strong roots. For best results, consider moving seedlings to a greenhouse, cold frame or outdoors once they germinate to give them the light and cooler conditions they need to thrive.

SEEDLING CARE

PRICKING OUT

Prick out your seedlings when they have developed their first set of true leaves. This is usually the second set after the initial seed leaves (*cotyledons*) and look like leaves that the parent plant will have.

Gently disturb the soil around the seedling, and hold the leaf (not the stem or roots, as damage to these parts can irrevocably damage the plant). Use your finger or pricking tool (I love the metal Sneeboer as pricker as shown, but a thin pen will work) to carefully level the seedling out from beneath. Be careful to keep the entire root system intact and not to bruise or snap the stem.

TRANSPLANTING SEEDLINGS

Make or 'dib' a hole in the centre of your new container or cell potting mix with your finger, pen or dibber.

Place the seedling in the hole, making sure the roots go down rather than curling upwards. You can put most of the stem into the hole too. Fill the hole and firm the soil gently around the base of the seedling to hold it in place.

Water the seedlings carefully after transplanting. The best way is to let them sit in a tray of water for an hour, or to spray with a fine mist to avoid washing away soil or damaging the young plants.

Place the seedlings in a well-lit area, avoiding intense direct sunlight and draughty spots to begin with to ensure they aren't too stressed by the move.

POTTING ON

As the plants grow, they'll eventually need more space. Once the roots have filled the pot, it is time for them to move on. We like to plant them out in the garden as soon as possible, but if you have trouble with pests like slugs who are hungry for tiny seedlings, or are planting in a spot with more mature plants, or have intense weather to contend with, you'll need to pot on, allow the seedling to get bigger and more robust before planting out.

Prepare a pot with potting soil, choosing a pot that is slightly larger than the current one. You won't need to fill it as the plant will take up a lot of the space.

Gently remove the plant from its existing pot or cell (shown below). You can gently squeeze or tap a pot to release the plug plant, or use a sharp tool down the edge of the pot to lever the root ball out. Place the plant in the new pot, ensuring it is the same depth as before. Fill in around the plant with more soil and gently firm it down. Place a water tray underneath or spray with a fine mist.

PINCHING OUT

Pinching out a seedling (shown above) is a simple technique used to encourage plants to grow bushier and produce more side stems, which will end up with more flowers. The main growing tip hogs the growth hormone, so once removed, the hormone can be spread further around the plant. Allow the seedlings to grow a few sets of true leaves. This is usually a month or so after germination.

Find the growing tip – this is the topmost part of the plant where new growth appears. It's the very tip of the central stem. Use clean sharp secateurs or your fingers to gently pinch off the growing tip just above a set of leaves. I like to pinch at around the halfway point of the plant. After pinching, make sure the plant has enough water and sunlight to help it recover and grow.

Single stemmed annuals, such as stocks, don't benefit from this, so check the requirements before you do so.

PROPAGATION FROM CUTTINGS

This method of propagating gives you a clone of the parent plant.

TAKING CUTTINGS

A great way to propagate your favourite plants and expand your garden, taking cuttings can be done in a number of ways, and the type of cutting you take is dependent on the type of plant you're propagating. You don't need to use rooting hormone, but it can help with the success rate. It comes in the form of powders and gels, or you can make your own.

WILLOW WATER

Making willow water is a simple and effective way to propagate plants using a natural rooting hormone.

Collect fresh willow branches (any variety of willow will work). Look for the young, flexible branches, as it's these that contain high levels of auxins, a natural plant hormone that promotes root growth.

Chop the branches into small pieces, around 2.5–5 cm (1–2 inches) long. This will help release the auxins into the water more effectively.

Place the willow pieces in a container filled with water. Let them soak for 24–48 hours, allowing the auxins to leach out into the water. Strain the liquid into a lidded container, and throw the branches on the compost heap.

To use the willow water as a rooting hormone. Simply dip each cut end of cutting into it before planting in soil. The water can be stored for up to two weeks.

TAKING ROOT CUTTINGS

Taking root cuttings is a great way to propagate plants. The steps are relatively straightforward, and the cuttings can be taken from a few herbaceous perennials and some shrubs. With just a small piece of root, you can grow entirely new plants, making this method an excellent way to increase your stock. Once you get the hang of it, you may find yourself scanning your garden for more candidates to try it on.

Paris and I have a favourite perennial from which to take a root cutting namely *Verbascum*. The 'Southern Charm' variety we love the most is expensive to grow from seed, so once we have good plants, we take cuttings to expand our collection.

Plenty of herbaceous plants can be propagated from root cuttings, including *Acanthus*, Japanese anemone, *Echinops*, *Papaver orientale* (oriental poppy), phlox and *Verbascum*.

The best time to take root cuttings is during the plant's dormant season, usually late autumn or winter, when the plant is not actively growing. Make sure you choose a healthy parent plant to take the cuttings from.

You will need:

- **Pair of secateurs, scissors or a knife:** Make sure these are clean and sharp
- **Container:** Filled with well-draining soil or a rooting medium, such as horticultural grit, perlite or vermiculite
- **Fork:** For loosening soil
- **Watering can with fine rose or spray bottle:** Ensures gentle watering

1. LIFT THE PLANT
Carefully remove the plant from the ground or pot without damaging the roots. A garden fork is good at loosening the soil. Shake off excess soil to expose the root system. Look for thick, healthy roots, ideally pencil-sized in diameter. Avoid damaged or diseased roots.

2. CUT THE ROOTS

Use your cutting tool to cut root segments into pieces about 5–10 cm (2–4 inches) long. Make straight cuts on the end closest to the crown, and angled cuts on the far end to help determine the top and bottom.

3. POT THE CUTTINGS

You can lay the cuttings horizontally or vertically into your prepared container, leaving the top just above the soil surface. If needed, cover the container lightly with soil.

4. WATERING

Water the cuttings gently. Keep them in a cool area with indirect light and maintain even moisture in the soil.

5. TRANSPLANTING

Roots will develop new shoots in a few weeks or months. Keeping the soil consistently moist and at a stable temperature is best. Once the cuttings have developed leaves and are strong enough, you can transplant them into pots or directly into the garden.

TAKING HARDWOOD CUTTINGS

Hardwood cuttings are taken from deciduous trees and plants in late autumn and through winter when they have no leaves left. This is the period when they are dormant, and it's the best time for taking a hardwood cutting.

Among the deciduous shrubs from which you can take cuttings are abelia, buddleia, cornus, forsythia, ribes, rose and viburnum, plus climbers, such as lonicera and jasmine, and from fruit such as currants, figs and gooseberries.

You will need:

- **Pair of secateurs, scissors or a knife:** Make sure these are clean and sharp
- **Hormone rooting powder or willow water (see page 156):** To encourage root growth
- **Potting compost**
- **Containers** (optional)

1. SELECT THE SHOOT

From your parent plant, select healthy-looking shoots. Cut off the soft growth at the tip of the plant. Cut the shoot into sections around 15–30 cm (6–12 inches) long each, cutting just above a bud. Dip the bottom (straight) end into the hormone rooting powder or willow water.

2. PLANT THE CUTTING

You can plant your cuttings either directly in the ground or grow them in containers. When planting, you want two-thirds of the cutting to be below the surface, as the roots will form here. The one-third above the ground should include at least one bud node.

If planting directly outdoors, position the plant in a sheltered spot with well-drained soil. Add some compost to your planting hole. Plant your cuttings 10–15 cm (4–6 inches) apart. You will need to keep them in place for a full year and water them well. If there is a very cold winter, they might need protection from a cold frame or cloche.

The other option is to plant your cuttings in containers filled with a combination of compost and potting grit. Keep the containers in a sheltered spot until the following year and water as needed.

TAKING BASAL CUTTINGS

Basal means from the bottom or base. This type of cutting takes new shoots from the base crown of a plant. You can take cuttings like this from herbaceous perennial flowers, such as *Penstemon*, lupin, dahlia, salvia, phlox and delphinium, as well as shrubs such as Hydrangea, currant and lavender. The usual time to take basal cuttings is in spring, when new shoots are appearing from the ground.

You will need:

- **Secateurs:** Sharp and sterilized with rubbing alcohol
- **Plastic bag (optional):** To keep cuttings moist
- **Small pot:** Filled with well-draining potting mix or a mixture of horticultural grit or perlite and multipurpose compost
- **Rooting hormone (optional)**

1. CHOOSE YOUR PLANT
• Select a healthy and vigorous plant that you want to propagate and choose a stem near the base that has plenty of healthy shoots. This stem should be thick, about the diameter of a pencil. Follow the chosen stem down to the base of the plant, where the stem meets the crown. You might need to push away the soil to find the place where they connect.

2. TAKE THE CUTTING
• Use really sharp and sterilized secateurs so you don't spread disease to the mother plant. Sever the stem from where it is connected to the crown. Make sure the cutting is about 10–15 cm (4–6 inches) long. You can place the shoots in a plastic bag if you aren't going to pot them immediately. This will help them to retain moisture and have a higher chance of rooting.

3. PREPARE THE CUTTING
• Remove any lower leaves from the cutting to expose any nodes (some plants don't have leaves from the shoot at this stage, so this step is optional). Pinch out the growing tip, as this will encourage the growth down into the roots rather than up to the tip.

4. APPLY THE ROOTING HORMONE
• If you wish, dip the cut end of the basal root cutting in rooting hormone or willow water (see page 156) to encourage root growth.

5. POT THE CUTTING
• Take the pot of well-draining potting mix and make a hole in it. Plant the cutting so that at least one node is buried beneath the surface. Gently firm the soil around the cutting. Many people find that there is a greater success rate when one side of the stem is touching the side of the pot, especially when using terracotta pots (it is generally thought that terracotta, which absorbs extra moisture, helps keep the area around the node just right for encouraging new roots to grow; the side contact also helps keep the cutting stable while it develops roots).

6. WATER THE CUTTING
• Water the cutting thoroughly and place the pot in a warm and humid environment, such as a greenhouse or under a plastic bag to retain moisture. Check the cutting regularly to make sure the soil remains moist but not waterlogged. Avoid direct sunlight, as it can cause the cutting to dry out.

7. PLANTING OUT
• After a few weeks, the cutting should start developing roots. Once roots have formed, the cutting can be transplanted into a larger pot or directly into the garden.

TAKING SOFTWOOD CUTTINGS

Cuttings of this type can be taken from a variety of plants, including some shrubs, such as hydrangeas and roses, herbs, such as mint and basil, as well as pelargoniums and sedums. As the name suggests, the cutting is taken from the soft part of the stem, not the woodier, more mature parts often found nearer the base of a plant.

Some soft stems root so easily that all you need to do is place the cutting in a glass of water. Try this with basil, succulents, mint, sedums and pelargoniums. In midsummer I cut bunches of mint for vases in my kitchen. Not only do they look lovely, smell delicious and are useful to pluck a leaf or two from to make tea, but after three weeks or so, they've all rooted in the water and I can replant them in the garden as new plants.

You will need:

- **Clean, sharp scissors**
- **Rooting hormone or willow water** (see page 156)
- **Pot of well-draining potting compost**
- **Heat mat and propagator lid (optional)**

1. CHOOSE YOUR CUTTING
It's best to do this in the morning when the plant is naturally full of fluid and transpiration is still low. Start by selecting a healthy, soft stem, that is pencil thick or just a little slimmer. Most of the time we choose stems that have no flowers, but have found that roses, in particular, whose flowers are just going over, are more likely to produce roots. If choosing stems with spent buds on it, remove them from the cutting before planting.

2. MAKE THE CUTTING
Using clean, sharp scissors, cut a 10–15-cm (4–6-inch) piece of the stem just below a leaf node/ bud. Remove any lower leaves to expose the nodes where roots will form. A helpful tip is to slice a little wound down the stem at the end of the cutting to try and encourage a few roots to grow out of the side of the stem, not just down.

3. USE THE ROOTING HORMONE
Next, dip the cut end of the stem in rooting hormone or willow water to encourage root growth.

6. PLANTING OUT

Once the cutting has developed a healthy root system, you can transplant it into a larger pot or directly into the garden.

4. PLANT THE CUTTING

Make a hole in the compost with a dibber or pencil. Insert the cutting base first, so that the lowest pair of leaves sits just above the soil surface. Firm gently to hold it in place. Some gardeners prefer to place one side of the stem against the inside edge of the pot for extra support. Water thoroughly so the compost settles around the stem.

5. CARE AND WATERING

Keep the cutting in a warm, humid spot and mist regularly to maintain even moisture. Avoid over-humid conditions for pelargoniums, as they are prone to rot. Use a propagator lid or heat mat if you want more control and faster rooting. Roots usually begin to form in 6–10 weeks. Check regularly and remove cuttings that show signs of rot or die back.

LAYERING PLANTS

Layering is a plant propagation technique where new plants are formed while still attached to the parent plant. Many plants such as ivy self-layer – you might have seen the little roots attaching themselves to trees and the ground. Layering can sometimes happen by accident in my garden, when plants such as cosmos get blown over in a strong wind; I'll come across them a few weeks later to find tiny new roots peeking out from where they have been bent to the ground. The fact that layering can happen by accident shows how easy it can be.

This technique is best done in spring or late summer when plants are in active growth, and patience is key as some plants take longer to root than others.

Plants that respond well to layering propagation techniques are numerous. **Examples:** acer, azalea, blackberries, boxwood, camellia, *Chaenomeles*, clematis, climbing hydrangea, cornus, cosmos, cotinus, daphne, forsythia, *Hamamelis*, hazel, honeysuckle, ivy, jasmine, lilac, magnolia, roses, snowberries, tomatoes, viburnum, and some raspberries.

HOW TO GROUND LAYER YOUNG

Select a healthy stem and choose a young, flexible and disease-free branch. Gently bend the stem down towards the soil and find a section that can lie flat on the ground. Lightly scrape the stem's underside to expose a bit of the inner tissue. You can apply a small amount of rooting hormone to speed up the process (this is optional).

Dig a shallow trench where the prepared stem meets the soil. Bury the wounded section and secure it with a bent piece of wire, stone or peg. Ensure the tip of the stem is exposed and pointing upwards.

Water and keep the soil moist but not waterlogged. Check for new root growth every few weeks. Once the layered section has developed its own roots (which can take a few months), cut it from the mother plant and transplant it carefully to its new location.

HOW TO AIR LAYER MATURE PLANTS

Select a healthy, mature branch. Make a wound in a ring around the bark, a technique called girdling, or make a slit. Apply rooting hormone to the wound and cover it with damp sphagnum moss. Wrap the moss securely with plastic wrap to hold in moisture, and secure both ends with twist ties. Keep the moss moist while you wait. Roots usually develop in a few weeks to a few months.

Once roots are visible through the moss, cut the branch below the rooted area and plant it in potting soil or directly into the garden.

HOW TO TIP LAYER

This is used for plants such as blackberries. We grow a lot of thornless blackberries along the fence line by the compost heap, which act to soften the fence, and of course the fruit is so delicious to use in ice creams and crumbles. 'Merton' (the thornless variety I love) is also excellent as a cut flower foliage for late-summer arrangements. Using tip layering, I have taken one plant and turned it into many. You can propagate infinitely this way, all through the growing season.

New little aerial roots start to grow straight from the tips of blackberries, black and purple raspberries and tomatoes, making layering a straightforward way to propagate.

Select a long, arching stem that can reach the ground. Bend the stem over and bury the tip a good few centimetres (inches) underground. Water if the ground is dry. Leave for a few months, until the stem has enough new roots to cut and replant elsewhere.

HOW TO PLANT BARE-ROOT PLANTS

Bare-root plants, whether roses, trees, or hedging, are a wonderfully practical choice. They're easier on the budget and lighter on the planet, needing fewer resources to grow and transport than container plants. Once in the ground, they settle quickly, sending roots deep into the soil and getting on with the business of establishing themselves. With a little patience, they'll reward you as the seasons turn, growing strongly and filling the garden with leaf and flower.

WHEN TO DO IT

Plant bare-root plants during their dormant season, typically late autumn to early spring, when growth has slowed, and the soil is still workable but not frozen. This is the time when plants can establish their root systems without needing to support leaves or flowers. Choose a calm, overcast day to plant, as extreme cold or harsh winds can stress the roots during planting.

HOW TO DO IT

Start by soaking the roots in water for 1–2 hours before planting to rehydrate them. Meanwhile, dig a hole wide enough to spread the roots comfortably and deep enough so that the plant sits at the same depth it grew previously (look for a subtle soil line on the stem as a guide).

Although optional, I often sprinkle a scoop of mycorrhizal fungi onto the roots or into the planting hole before adding the plant. These beneficial fungi form a symbiotic relationship with the plant, extending its root system and helping it absorb water and nutrients more efficiently. They can significantly improve establishment and growth, particularly in poorer soils.

Place the plant in the hole, spreading out the roots gently to avoid tangling. Backfill the hole with soil, firming it gently as you go to eliminate air pockets. Water thoroughly to help the soil settle around the roots. For extra support, you can stake large bare-root trees or shrubs to protect them from wind as they establish.

DIVIDING PLANTS

Dividing perennials is a useful method to make more plants, and a way to rejuvenate the mother plant and control the size. Even if you don't want to make more plants, you can also consider the plant's shape and condition, and if a plant looks crowded or performs poorly, it might benefit from division.

WHEN TO DO IT

The best time to divide perennials that bloom in the summer is during the spring.

HOW TO DO IT

Prepare the plant for division by watering it well a few days before. This will make it easier to lift. Use a garden fork to loosen around the plant, ensuring to keep some distance from the base of the plant itself. Gently lift it out of the ground, making sure you include as much of the root ball as possible.

If the plant is small and pliable enough, you can use your hands to gently tease the roots apart to make smaller plants from the single large one.

Another option to use on bigger, denser plants is to cut them with a knife or a spade; this is especially useful if working with heavy clay or if the root ball is tightly bound. Lay the root ball on its side, split the crown in half and repeat the process until you have the number of pieces you want. You can also put two forks back to back in the centre of the clump and pull them apart.

Remove any dead foliage or damaged roots before planting the divisions as soon as possible, at the same depth as the original plant. Keep the plants well watered while they settle in.

DIVIDING BULBS

You can also divide certain bulbs, such as snowdrops (see above and right), when they're in flower or just finished flowering, what gardeners call 'in the green'. This method works for bluebells, snowdrops, winter aconites, daffodils, lily of the valley, *Muscari*, *Leucojum*, and crocuses.

HOW TO DIVIDE BULBS

1. WAIT UNTIL FLOWERING IS OVER
The best time to divide in the green is when the flowers start to fade but the leaves are still green and healthy, but you can still move them successfully when in full flower (see pictures). The bulbs are still in the process of storing energy for next year, so you must treat the roots with the upmost care.

2. LIFT THE CLUMP GENTLY
Using a hand fork or spade, carefully dig around the clump and lift it from the soil, taking care not to damage the roots or bulbs.

3. TEASE APART SMALLER SECTIONS
With your hands, gently separate the clump into smaller groups, each with a few bulbs and some leafy growth still attached.

4. REPLANT STRAIGHT AWAY
Plant each new group back into the soil at the same depth they were growing before, spacing them a little apart to give them room to settle and multiply.

5. WATER WELL
Give them a good soak after planting to help them re-establish.

HOW TO PLANT BULBS

Planting bulbs is one of the simplest ways to add bursts of seasonal colour to your garden. Tuck them into the soil at the right time, and they'll reward you with fresh leaves and flowers just when you need them most.

Spring-flowering bulbs (e.g. tulips, daffodils): Plant in autumn to early winter, from September to December. I get my narcissi in before the first frosts. Tulips can be planted later, preferably after the first frost, as long as the ground is not frozen

Summer-flowering bulbs (e.g. lilies, gladioli): Plant in spring, after the danger of frost has passed.

1. PREPARE THE AREA
Choose a sunny, well-drained location. Most bulbs dislike waterlogged soil, so if your garden soil is heavy, consider adding grit or using raised beds or containers. **Exceptions:** Bulbs such as snakeshead fritillaries and camassias thrive in damp conditions.

2. DIG THE HOLE
Use the rule of planting bulbs at a depth of 2–3 times their height. Space bulbs according to their variety, generally 5–15 cm (2–6 inches) apart.

3. POSITION THE BULBS
Place bulbs with the pointed end facing up (this is the growing tip) and the flatter, rounded end (where roots will grow) facing down.

4. ADD FERTILIZER
Optional, but a little fertilizer sprinkled into the planting hole encourages strong growth.

5. COVER AND WATER
Gently backfill the hole with soil, firming it lightly to remove air pockets. Water thoroughly after planting to settle the soil and initiate root growth.

6. ADD MULCH
Optional, but a layer of mulch will insulate the bulbs during winter and suppress weeds.

PROTECTING YOUR BULBS FROM WILDLIFE

Bulbs can be vulnerable to various creatures that may damage or destroy them.

- **Squirrels, mice and voles:** These animals dig up bulbs for food.
- **Slugs and snails:** Feed on tender shoots as they emerge.
- **Insects (e.g. narcissus bulb fly):** Larvae burrow into bulbs, causing decay.

Here's how to protect your bulbs:

Inspect bulbs before planting: Discard any soft, mouldy or damaged bulbs, as they are more susceptible to the ravages of hungry creatures and disease.

Use barriers: Cover bulbs with wire mesh or chicken wire after planting to prevent digging. Remove it when shoots appear. Place bulbs in pots or raised beds to deter burrowing from less welcome creatures.

Choose resistant bulbs: If you live in a hotspot for wildlife and can't put up preventative fencing, then opt for pest-resistant varieties, such as daffodils, alliums or fritillaries, which are less appealing to wildlife.

Apply repellents: Use organic repellents to deter rodents and insects. We often scatter some garlic granules (like the ones used in equine food) around planted bulbs, as the strong smell seems to put creatures off.

Plant deeply: Bury bulbs slightly deeper than recommended to make them harder for those less welcome creatures to access.

PROTECTING SHOOTS AND BLOOMS

Slugs and snails: Use beer traps, copper tape or organic slug pellets to protect emerging shoots. You can also go out at night and hand-pick them off the plants or try nematodes for slugs.

Physical barriers: Surround young plants with crushed eggshells or gravel to deter slugs and snails. If the molluscs are abundant it's better to plant bulbs in pots and put them in harder-to-reach areas.

HOW TO GET A SUCCESSION OF FLOWERS FROM BULBS

Layering bulbs in your garden, even in pots, allows you to enjoy a continuous display of blooms throughout the seasons. By layering, you'll create a dynamic and ever-changing display, with new flowers appearing as others fade. This is an easy and impactful way to add depth movement, and interest to your garden.

Narcissus 'Tête-à-Tête'

MY FAVOURITE SUCCESSION BULBS

For an almost continuous supply of flowers, I love:

Late winter

- Snowdrops
- *Leucojum*
- Crocus (early, mid-season and late varieties)
- *Iris reticulata*

Early spring

- *Muscari*
- *Narcissus* (early, mid-season and late varieties)

Late spring

- Tulip (early, mid-season and late varieties)
- Ranunculus
- Allium (early, mid-season varieties)

Early summer

- Honey garlic
- Iris
- Camassia

Late summer

- Lily (including martagon varieties)
- Gladioli

Autumn – early winter

- Nerine
- Crocus
- Cyclamen

1. ARRANGE BY FLOWERING TIME
Place the largest, latest-flowering bulbs as the bottom layer. Add smaller, earlier-flowering bulbs as you move upwards.

2. PLANT SLIGHTLY APART
Space bulbs 2.5–3 cm (1–1½ inches) apart, slightly farther than you would for a single layer. This ensures each bulb has enough room to thrive.

3. ADD SOIL BETWEEN LAYERS
Cover each layer with 5 cm (2 inches) of soil or potting compost before adding the next layer.

4. PLANT DEEPER THAN THE BULB'S HEIGHT
For optimal growth, plant bulbs at a depth three times their height, and space them three times their width apart.

LAYERING WITH EARLY AND LATE-SEASON BULBS

When layering planting in a garden I am frequently drawn to bulbs, whether that's a carpet of snowdrops under a tree, or reliably perennial tulips (see page 108 for cutting garden recipe) bringing some much-needed post-winter colour in a spring border. I can't say it enough: I really believe that bulbs are essential for creating a layered look that lasts through the year. They're incredibly versatile and easy to incorporate into almost any part of your garden. I love tucking bulbs between shrubs and perennials, at the base of trees, and even along hedges. They take up minimal space, and their foliage dies back later in the season, allowing other plants to shine.

Bulbs are particularly valuable for adding interest during quieter times of the year – early spring and late autumn – when the garden might otherwise feel sparse. One of the best things about bulbs is that you can keep adding or dividing them year after year. As your borders mature and you identify gaps in your seasonal display, bulbs become a simple yet effective solution to extend interest across all seasons.

Try this: Choose early bloomers, such as snowdrops or 'February Gold' narcissi to brighten the start of the year. For late-season beauty, go for *Crocus pulchellus* or *Cyclamen cilicium* to keep the layers flowering well into autumn.

HOW TO SAVE SEEDS

What could be easier and more satisfying than plundering your plants' seed heads for hundreds of potential new plants.

Saving seeds allows gardeners to preserve plant varieties, save money and ensure future plantings are adapted to local conditions. It also contributes to sustainability and self-sufficiency.

The thing I love most about seeds is that each seed carries more than the promise of new life; it holds a story. A sunflower grown year after year in the same garden learns the quirks of its soil, the rhythm of its rain, the warmth of its sun. Over time, it adapts, subtly shifting to thrive a little better. These small changes are acts of survival wrapped up in beautiful petals. Seeds become living archives of their surroundings, etching their environment's struggles and triumphs into their genes.

One of the most delightful aspects of saving seeds is the ability to share them. Exchanging seeds with friends, family or local gardening groups fosters community and allows you to experiment with new varieties.

Nigella (love-in-a-mist) seeds

WHEN TO DO IT

Collect seeds when they are fully mature. This is typically after their flowering and fruiting stages, when pods are dry and starting to split, the seeds are rattling in the seedpod, or when seeds easily detach from plants.

HOW TO DO IT

1. COLLECT THE SEEDS

Select healthy, disease-free plants for seed saving, prioritizing open-pollinated or heirloom varieties, as hybrid seeds may not produce offspring true to type. When the seeds are ready for harvest, cut the seed heads or pods from the plant once they are dry, and place them in a paper bag. For fleshy fruits, such as tomatoes, scoop out the seeds and rinse them in water to remove any pulp.

2. DRY THE SEEDS

Spread the seeds on kitchen paper or a screen in a cool, dry location, and allow them to air-dry completely, which may take several days. Once dried, remove as much non-seed material as possible. This process often involves threshing (breaking the seeds loose from stalks and seed heads) and winnowing (separating seeds from plant debris). Threshing can be done manually by hand or foot, while winnowing typically involves using buckets and the wind to blow away lighter chaff, leaving the seeds clean and ready for storage.

A NOTE ON STORING SEEDS

Storing seeds properly is one of the simplest yet most rewarding steps you can take to ensure a thriving garden year after year.

Seed viability varies significantly between species. Some seeds, such as those of lotus plants, can remain viable for hundreds of years, while others, such as carrot seeds, may retain excellent germination for only a year or so. Research the specific seeds you want to save to understand their viability and storage needs. Proper handling and storage are essential to maximize their lifespan.

WHY STORE SEEDS?

Seeds are tiny powerhouses of potential, and proper storage keeps them viable for as long as possible. Although some seeds can last almost indefinitely, many, without the right conditions, can lose their ability to germinate, leaving you with disappointment instead of lush, healthy plants. By understanding and applying a few basic principles, you can extend the life of your seeds and enjoy their benefits for seasons to come.

THE BASICS OF SEED STORAGE

Dryness is key: Seeds need to stay dry to prevent mould, rot and premature germination. Before storing, ensure seeds are thoroughly dried. You can lay them out on paper or a mesh screen in a cool, airy spot for a week or two after collecting. Remember seeds are living things, so you don't want to dehydrate them completely, just get them dried out.

Cool and consistent temperatures: Seeds prefer cool, stable temperatures. Aim to store them in a location that stays around 5–10°C (41–50°F), such as a refrigerator or a garden shed. Avoid conditions that fluctuate too much, such as in a greenhouse.

Darkness is essential: Exposure to light can slowly reduce a seed's viability. Use opaque containers or keep your storage jars and packets in a dark place, such as a cupboard or a lidded box.

Airtight and organized: Store seeds in airtight containers, such as small glass jars, zip-top bags, or purpose-made seed packets. Add silica gel packets to absorb moisture if you're in a humid environment. Label each container clearly with the plant name, variety and collection date.

TIPS FOR LONGEVITY

Test for viability: If you're unsure about older seeds, test their germination by placing a few on damp kitchen paper and keeping them warm. If they sprout, they're still viable.

Rotate your stock: Use older seeds first and replenish your collection regularly to ensure freshness.

HOW TO ESTABLISH A WILDFLOWER MEADOW

Wildflower meadows are invaluable for supporting biodiversity, providing food and habitats for pollinators, such as bees, butterflies and other wildlife. They require less maintenance than traditional lawns, improve soil health and add natural beauty to your garden.

One of the most rewarding aspects of establishing a meadow is watching it evolve over time, seeing new species emerge naturally. While letting grass grow long and observing which wild flowers appear is a wonderful approach, there are ways to speed up the process and encourage a more diverse array of wild flowers.

HOW TO DO IT

1. CHOOSE THE SITE

Select a sunny location with well-draining soil, as most wild flowers prefer these conditions, and avoid nutrient-rich soil, which encourages grasses and weeds to outcompete wild flowers.

2. PREPARE THE GROUND

Strip the turf entirely to expose bare soil. This creates a blank canvas for sowing wildflower seeds, minimizing competition from existing vegetation. Clear the area of weeds and debris. Lightly rake or till the soil to create a fine, crumbly seedbed. Avoid overworking the soil, as wild flowers thrive in low-fertility conditions.

3. REDUCE GRASS DOMINANCE

Grass can hinder wildflower growth, and in large areas, where it's impossible to remove the grass, you can suppress it instead by introducing yellow rattle (*Rhinanthus minor*), a semi-parasitic plant that feeds on grass roots and reduces its vigour, creating space for wild flowers to thrive. Sow yellow rattle seeds in autumn, as they require winter stratification to germinate.

4. SELECT AND SOW SEEDS

Choose a wildflower seed mix tailored to your soil type and region. Opt for native species to support local ecosystems. Mix seeds with sand to ensure even distribution, then broadcast the mixture across the soil.

5. PRESS SEEDS INTO THE SOIL

Gently roll over or tread on the area to press seeds into the soil. Do not bury them deeply; many wildflower seeds require light to germinate.

6. WATER SPARINGLY

Water only if the weather is unusually dry. Overwatering may encourage weed growth and inhibit wildflower establishment.

PATIENCE AND MAINTENANCE

First-year growth: Be patient; many wild flowers take time to establish. In the first year, plants often focus on root development, with blooms appearing more abundantly in subsequent years.

Weed control: Regularly remove invasive weeds to give wild flowers space to thrive. Be careful not to disturb young wildflower seedlings.

Cutting the meadow: Cutting a wildflower meadow helps maintain its diversity by preventing aggressive grasses or plants from dominating. It also allows seeds to disperse and encourages new growth.

When to cut: Late summer to early autumn (August to September). Cut after wild flowers have set seed and the seeds have been dispersed.

Optional second cut: For meadows with vigorous grasses, a light cut in early spring can suppress grass growth and promote wild flowers.

How to cut: Use a scythe, mower or strimmer set to 10–15 cm (4–6 inches) to avoid damaging wildlife and young plants. Leave the cuttings for 1–2 weeks to allow seeds to drop back into the soil. Collect and compost clippings to reduce soil fertility and prevent smothering new growth.

Note: Consider adding fruit trees and bulbs to your meadow for a perfectly layered, wildlife-friendly, seasonal garden.

Red campion (*Silene dioica*)

CARING FOR YOUR GARDEN

INTEREST THROUGH THE SEASONS

A question I'm often asked is how to create a garden that offers interest all year round. The key is thinking beyond just flowers and considering a plant's form, texture and how it changes throughout the year. While flowers bring obvious beauty through colour and scent, the enduring interest comes from the structure, patterns and contrasts that plants offer in every season.

If you're unfamiliar with a plant, it can be hard to visualize how it behaves throughout the year. Thankfully, books and the internet are invaluable resources for researching a plant's 'seasonal personality'. I find a visual approach works best. When planning a border, I collect images of plants I'm considering – online or from catalogues – and group them by the seasons to which they offer interest. If one season feels underwhelming, I add more plants for that time of year. Remember, seasonal interest doesn't have to come solely from flowers – it could be vibrant foliage, berries or captivating textures.

Bulbs are especially useful for filling seasonal gaps, as they can be layered among shrubs and perennials. Hardy biennials, such as aquilegias and foxgloves, or annuals, such as cosmos and snapdragons, are also excellent for filling spaces with long-lasting colour. When waiting for a border to mature, I often tuck in a few annuals to create a sense of abundance while the permanent plants establish themselves.

A NOTE ON SEASONS

Recently someone asked me how to know when spring has come and that it is the right time to start sowing seeds. It's a really good question, and one that can't be answered succinctly. It takes a mixture of using three ways we humans have come up with to track the changing seasons, each offering unique insights.

ASTRONOMICAL SEASONS

These are based on the Earth's position relative to the sun, marked by solstices and equinoxes.

Northern hemisphere:

Spring equinox: 20 March
Summer solstice: 21 June
Autumn equinox: 22 September
Winter solstice: 21 December

Southern hemisphere:

Spring equinox: 22 September
Summer solstice: 21 December
Autumn equinox: 20 March
Winter solstice: 21 June

METEOROLOGICAL SEASONS

Dividing the year into equal three-month blocks makes it easier to track seasonal weather patterns.

Northern hemisphere:

Spring: 1 March–31 May
Summer: 1 June–31 August
Autumn: 1 September–30 November
Winter: 1 December–28 February

Southern hemisphere:

Spring: 1 September–30 November
Summer: 1 December–28 February
Autumn: 1 March–31 May
Winter: 1 June–31 August

PHENOLOGICAL INDICATORS

Phenology is the study of recurring phenomena, especially as influenced by climatic conditions. Although I rely upon the calendar for scheduling and planning ahead with tasks, my favourite method of telling if it's time to do seasonal jobs involves observing natural signs of seasonal change. The weather has become more erratic in growing seasons around the world, so I rely more readily on nature's indicators for cues on when to do my seasonal jobs. By observing these signs, you can align your gardening activities with nature's rhythm, making the most of each season's opportunities.

Trees and shrubs: Look for leaf buds, flowering, fruit ripening and leaf fall.

Flowers: The first blooms signal winter's end, while frost hints at its return.

Migratory birds: Arrival, nesting and departure patterns offer clues about seasonal shifts.

Planting cues: For example, dandelions in bloom suggest it's time to plant potatoes, while hardy annual seeds sprouting in the soil indicate that it's safe to start direct sowing.

PHENOLOGICAL PROVERBS

There are many ancient proverbs and sayings that are rich in gardening wisdom, often tied to seasonal changes and agricultural rhythms. Some of my favourite proverbs, rooted in observation, offer both practical advice and a connection to the rhythms of nature. I've sprinkled some seasonal ones throughout the next sections for your enjoyment. Here are a few to start with:

'One for the rook, one for the crow,
one to rot, and one to grow.'

A traditional planting rhyme reminding gardeners to sow extra seeds to account for losses.

'Make hay while the sun shines.'

An encouragement to take advantage of good weather for essential gardening or farming tasks.

'When the hawthorn blooms, sow your corn soon.'

Hawthorn flowers signal the soil is warm enough for sowing crops such as corn. I also love that the traditional way to tell if the soil is warm enough is to pull your trousers down and sit on it with a bare bottom! If you can't feel a chill, it's time. Although I don't do this personally, it reminds me to go out and feel the soil with my hands!

'If it's time to weed, then it's time to seed.'

When the seeds drop from the plant and start germinating, it's time to follow that plant's cue and do some sowing of your own.

SPRING

'April showers bring May flowers.'

This well-known saying highlights how spring rain is essential for abundant blooms later in the season.

Spring begins with the unfurling of green buds, blossoms and vibrant bulbs. I plant as many *Narcissus* varieties as I can – favourites, such as 'Thalia', 'Actaea' and 'Tête-à-Tête', are reliable and perennialise well. Tulips are another spring staple, especially species tulips and hybrids, such as 'Batalinii Bronze Charm' and 'Spring Green'. Including a mix of bulbs ensures continuous colour and beauty as the season unfolds.

SEASONAL HIGHLIGHTS

Bulbs: Crocus, *Leucojum*, *Iris reticulata*, *Narcissus*

Perennials: *Primula*, hellebore, lungwort, *Tellima grandiflora*, *Silene dioica*, *Gillenia trifoliata*, *Heuchera*, lupin

Biennials: Wallflowers, aquilegia, angelica

Shrubs: Daphne, camellia, ribes, physocarpus, *Spiraea thunbergii*, forsythia

Trees: Crab apple, cherry blossom, *Davidia involucrata*, magnolia ('Stellata' is especially lovely for small gardens)

Opposite: Narcissus 'Erlicheer'

Muscari 'Babies Breath'

EARLY SPRING: GARDEN JOBS

- **Plant bare-root trees and shrubs:** Finish planting bare root specimens before they break dormancy.
- **Sow hardy annuals:** Sow hardy annuals under cover, or once the soil warms slightly; direct sow seeds that like cold stratification, such as larkspur.
- **Lift and divide snowdrops**: Move snowdrops while they're still 'in the green' to new areas.
- **Lift and divide overcrowded perennials**: Split clumps of established perennials, such as hostas and daylilies, to rejuvenate them and create more plants.
- **Weed and mulch**: Pull emerging weeds, and mulch areas you did not mulch over the winter to suppress regrowth and retain moisture in the coming months.
- **Clean water butts and gutters**: Clear debris to ensure efficient water collection during spring rains.
- **Plant summer-flowering bulbs**: Add gladiolus, lilies and alliums to your garden for vibrant summer displays.
- **Top-dress containers**: Refresh the top layer of compost in pots with nutrient-rich material to support healthy growth.
- **Install plant supports**: Place supports early for tall plants, such as delphiniums and peonies, to avoid disturbing their roots later.
- **Re-lay or check irrigation systems**: In annual beds, or any areas where mulch was added, re-lay irrigation systems to ensure proper placement. Check for clogs or leaks, as these systems might have been disturbed during mulching or seasonal changes.

LATE SPRING: GARDEN JOBS

- **Sow summer annuals**: Sow less hardy annuals, such as cosmos and marigolds.
- **Prune spring-flowering shrubs**: Cut back shrubs, such as forsythia and flowering currants, after they bloom to shape them.
- **Stake tall perennials**: Provide early support to plants such as delphiniums and peonies to prevent damage from wind or rain.
- **Harden off young plants**: Gradually acclimatize seedlings and tender plants to outdoor conditions by moving them outside during the day.
- **Deadhead spring bulbs**: Remove spent flowers from daffodils and tulips to prevent them from setting seed. This allows the plant to put the energy back into the bulb. Allow their foliage to die back naturally.
- **Feed hungry plants:** If you decide you'd like to feed your garden, you can apply a seaweed dilution or comfrey tea (see page 204) to flowering plants, such as roses, and fruiting vegetables to encourage blooms and crops.
- **Mow lawns regularly**: Start mowing the lawn, gradually lowering the cutting height to encourage healthy growth.
- **Watch for less welcome creatures**: Look out for aphids and caterpillars, removing them by hand or with organic treatments such as nemotodes.
- **Do a weed strike**: Now is the time to keep on top of the weeds. As the soil warms, the seeds in the soil will germinate. Some you might want there, some you might not. Run a hoe over the soil surface and dig out the roots of any perennial weeds, such as dock and bindweed.

SUMMER

'A dry May and a dripping June brings all things into tune.'

A dry late spring followed by wet early summer is ideal for crops and gardens.

Summer is a time of abundance. Repeat-flowering roses and herbaceous perennials offer long-lasting blooms, while summer bulbs, such as alliums and martagon lilies, add striking vertical accents. With so many options, summer borders can be both diverse and dazzling.

SEASONAL HIGHLIGHTS

Bulbs: Alliums, martagon lilies, camassia, Siberian iris, bearded iris

Perennials: Lavender, salvia, nepeta, hardy geraniums, astrantia, achillea, *Verbena hastata*, *Phlomis russeliana*, *Verbascum*, linaria, campanula, *Gillenia trifoliata*

Biennials: Foxgloves, sweet rocket, honesty, sweet williams, teasels

Shrubs: Roses, hydrangea, *Philadelphus*, deutzia, cotinus, *Physocarpus*

Trees: *Amelanchier*, *Calycanthus*, kousa

Grasses: *Miscanthus*, *Molinia*, *Briza*, *Deschampia*, stipa, anemanthele, carex, *Melica altissima* 'Atropurpurea', *Melica altissima* 'Alba', *Pennisetum*

Creepers: *Erigeron*, creeping thyme

Cut flowers: Cosmos, sweet peas, calendula, *Nigella*, cornflowers, *Panicum violaceum*, zinnias, dahlias, snapdragons, sunflowers

Opposite: Roses 'Roald Dahl', 'Port Sunlight', 'Litchfield Angel' and 'Iceberg'

Geranium 'Rozanne'

EARLY SUMMER: GARDEN JOBS

- **Deadhead flowers:** Remove spent blooms on roses, sweet pea and annuals to encourage repeat flowering.
- **The Chelsea chop**: A pruning technique performed in late May and early June in the northern hemisphere (around the time of the Chelsea Flower Show) to encourage bushier growth and later flowering. Cut back perennials, such as sedum and helenium, by one-third to half their height. This delays blooms and creates a more compact plant with stronger stems and more flowers. For variety, chop some stems but leave others untouched for a staggered display.
- **Pinch out tips**: Pinch out the growing tips of seedlings such as cosmos and snapdragons to promote bushier growth and more flowers.
- **Harvest early crops**: If you're cultivating fruit, vegetables and flowers, start picking! Early summer favourites, such as sweet peas, roses and strawberries, are ready to be enjoyed.
- **Check mulch levels:** Reapply mulch where needed to retain moisture and keep roots cool.
- **Plant out tender flowers and vegetables:** Transplant plants, such as tomatoes, courgettes and zinnias into their final positions once the risk of frost has passed.
- **Weed regularly:** Stay on top of weeds to reduce competition for water and nutrients.
- **Water regularly**: Keep an eye on moisture levels, especially in pots and newly planted areas. Water early in the morning or late in the evening.
- **Feed plants**: If you are feeding your plants, continue to do so on a weekly basis.
- **Stake tall plants**: Support fast-growing plants, such as delphiniums, to prevent them from flopping.
- **Thin out fruit trees**: Remove excess fruit from apples and pears to ensure larger, healthier crops.
- **Deadhead regularly**: Snip spent flowers off annuals and perennials to prolong flowering.
- **Check for less welcome creatures**: Inspect for slugs, snails and aphids, and take action to keep them under control.
- **Collect seeds**: Gather seeds from late spring-flowering plants, such as aquilegia and foxgloves. You can sprinkle them in gaps around the garden or sow them in trays.

LATE SUMMER: GARDEN JOBS

- **Prune summer-flowering shrubs:** Trim shrubs, such as lavender and hebes, after flowering to keep them tidy, or into the shapes and sizes you like.
- **Cut back perennials:** Deadhead and cut back spent stems to tidy borders and encourage fresh blooms.
- **Take cuttings:** Propagate tender plants, such as pelargoniums and salvias, to overwinter indoors in case you have a harsh winter.
- **Prepare for autumn planting:** Order spring-flowering bulbs and plan for any bare-root plants you want to add later in the year.
- **Check compost heaps:** Turn and water compost heaps to speed up decomposition during warm weather months.
- **Harvest crops**: Keep enjoying any flowers and vegetables you've grown for picking.
- **Sow biennials**: Plant seeds for biennials, such as foxgloves, sweet williams and wallflowers for blooms next year.
- **Trim hedges**: Tidy up hedges, but be mindful of nesting birds – wait until later if you suspect nests are present.
- **Feed and mulch beds**: Give borders a boost with a general-purpose fertilizer and a layer of mulch to retain moisture.
- **Collect seeds**: Gather seeds from early summer annuals, such as poppies and nigella, for future sowing.
- **Cut back spent perennials**: Trim back tired plants to encourage a second flush of growth or flowers.
- **Plan autumn planting:** Begin planning for autumn planting, such as spring bulbs and bare-root shrubs.
- **Order bulbs:** Get ahead by ordering spring-flowering bulbs, such as tulips, daffodils and hyacinths, for autumn planting. Ordering early ensures the best selection and gives you time to prepare planting spots in your garden.

AUTUMN

'Plant trees in the fall and their roots will call.'

Planting trees in autumn allows them to establish roots before winter dormancy.

Autumn brings a wealth of textures, seed heads, berries and fiery foliage. One of my favourites is the spindle tree, with its sunset-hued leaves and bright pink and orange berries. Late-flowering asters, such as 'Little Carlow' and 'Prince', can keep colour in the garden well into the cooler months, proving that autumn doesn't have to rely solely on earthy tones.

SEASONAL HIGHLIGHTS

Bulbs/Tubers: *Colchicum* (autumn crocus), nerines, cyclamen

Perennials: Asters, sedum, Japanese anemones, hardy geraniums, rudbeckia

Shrubs: Cotinus, viburnum, *Euonymus alatus*, physocarpus, *Spiraea thunbergii*

Trees: Acer (Japanese maple), crab apple, apple, *Amelanchier*

Grasses: *Briza*, *Deschampia*, stipa, *miscanthus*, carex, *Melica altissima* 'Atropurpurea', *M. altissima* 'Alba', *Pennisetum*

Cut flowers: Cosmos, zinnias, sunflowers, dahlias

Opposite: Dahlia 'Brown Sugar' and *Ammi majus* (Queen Anne's lace)

EARLY AUTUMN: GARDEN JOBS

- **Divide and transplant hardy perennials:** Split clumps of established perennials to rejuvenate them and create more plants. Dig them up carefully and replant in well-prepared soil.
- **Order bare-root roses**: Bare-root roses are affordable and establish well when planted in late autumn, winter or early spring. Ordering early ensures the best selection.
- **Plant narcissi**: Daffodil bulbs need to be at least twice their depth in well-drained soil to ensure cheerful blooms in spring.
- **Plant crocus**: Tuck crocus bulbs into borders or lawns for vibrant early spring colour. Plant in clusters about 7–10 cm (3–4 inches) deep for natural-looking drifts.
- **Plant evergreen shrubs**: Establish new evergreen shrubs while the soil is still warm, giving them time to root before winter.
- **Remove diseased leaves**: Clear away leaves with signs of disease, such as black spot or powdery mildew, to reduce overwintering spores.
- **Remove weeds**: Weed borders thoroughly to reduce competition for nutrients and stop weeds from setting seed.
- **Compost**: Add fallen leaves and plant material to your compost heap, avoiding diseased or woody material.
- **Check tools**: Clean, sharpen and oil tools to keep them in good working order for the tasks ahead.
- **Collect seeds**: Gather seeds from your annuals.
- **Start clearing annuals:** Begin clearing annuals that have gone over to make space for sowing some hardy annuals directly into the soil.
- **Start sowing hardy annuals**: Sow hardy annuals by planting seeds directly into prepared soil or seed trays, as they can tolerate cooler temperatures and will establish early for vibrant blooms later in the season.

LATE AUTUMN: GARDEN JOBS

- **Plant bare-root trees:** Choose a calm day and ensure the tree roots are spread out in a spacious, well-dug hole with added organic matter.
- **Enjoy seed heads**: Leave attractive seed heads, on plants such as alliums and ornamental grasses for winter interest and to support wildlife.
- **Plant bare-root shrubs**: These shrubs, which include roses, are economical and easy to plant. Position them in well-prepared soil with good drainage.
- **Plant perennials**: Planting new perennials now gives them time to settle in before winter. Mulch around the base for added protection.
- **Plant fritillaria bulbs**: Do this in well-draining soil. Fritillaria's unique bell-shaped flowers make a striking statement in spring.
- **Plant forced bulbs for a midwinter pick-me-up**: Pot up hyacinths, amaryllis or paperwhite narcissi indoors for fragrant and uplifting winter blooms.
- **Plant trees**: Autumn is the ideal time to plant trees. Dig a generous hole, stake the tree securely and water well.
- **Prune**: Tidy up summer-flowering shrubs and remove dead or damaged branches from trees and shrubs.
- **Clear**: Rake up fallen leaves, especially from lawns, and add them to your compost heap or make leaf mould (see page 203).
- **Deal with perennial weeds**: Dig out stubborn perennial weeds, ensuring you remove the entire root to prevent regrowth.
- **Put pots onto feet**: Raise pots slightly off the ground with pot feet (see page 215) to improve drainage and prevent waterlogging.
- **Bring tender plants under cover**: Move tender perennials, such as geraniums and fuchsias, to a frost-free space, perhaps a greenhouse or conservatory.
- **Lift dahlias**: If you live on heavy soil or in a particularly cold climate, carefully dig up dahlia tubers after the first frost blackens their foliage. Gently clean off excess soil, let them dry and store them in a cool, frost-free space over winter to protect them from freezing temperatures.
- **Sow sweet peas**: Best grown in pots or modules under cover in late autumn to give them a head start. Overwinter them in a cool, frost-free place, and you'll enjoy stronger plants and earlier blooms next spring. Unlike winter or spring-sown sweet peas, there's no need to pinch out those sown in autumn.
- **Sow hardy annuals**: Continue sowing hardy annuals by planting seeds directly into prepared soil or seed trays.

WINTER

'As the days lengthen, the cold strengthens.'

This proverb refers to the deep cold often experienced after the winter solstice, even as the days slowly grow longer.

These days I find myself drawn to the garden more in winter than in summer. I've come to appreciate the slower, quieter contributions it ushers in – the sharp geometry of frost etched on bare branches, the low, golden light filtering through the trees, green shoots pushing through snow. Winter interest comes from evergreen structures, paired with early-flowering bulbs and shrubs. Cyclamen, snowdrops, crocus, *Iris reticulata* and early *Narcissus* can leapfrog their bloom times to keep things lively. Evergreen, such as *Sarcococca*, add both structure and fragrance, their sweetly scented winter flowers providing a hint of spring in the air.

SEASONAL HIGHLIGHTS

Bulbs: Early snowdrops, early *Leucojum*, cyclamen

Perennials: Hellebores, heuchera

Perennial seedheads: Phlomis, foxgloves, *Eryngium yuccifolium*, asters, *Allium nigrum*, rudbeckia, honesty, sedum, achillea, sidalcea

Shrubs: Dogwood, *Chimonanthus praecox*, *Lonicera fragrantissima*

Evergreen shrubs: *Pittosporum*, hebe, mahonia, daphne, choisya, bay, boxwood, yew, *Euonymus*, *Osmanthus*, *Elaeagnus*, holly, *Sarcococca* (sweet box), *Viburnum tinus*

Trees: Birch, witch hazel, *Garrya elliptica*, hazel, *Chaenomeles speciosa*

Opposite: Rudbeckia seed heads

EARLY WINTER: GARDEN JOBS

- **Plant bare-root roses:** These need well-prepared soil to establish strong roots before spring growth.
- **Prune deciduous trees and shrubs:** Remove dead, damaged or crossing branches to shape and promote healthy growth.
- **Protect pots and containers**: Wrap pots with fleece to insulate roots from frost and prevent cracking.
- **Mulch beds and borders**: Apply a thick layer of compost, bark or well-rotted manure to protect roots and improve soil structure.
- **Feed birds**: Set up feeders and provide fresh water to support garden birds through the colder months.
- **Clean and sharpen tools:** Clean blades, sharpen edges and oil hinges to prepare tools for the spring rush.
- **Protect tender plants**: Wrap tender shrubs with fleece or hessian to shield them from frost and cold winds.
- **Move containers to sheltered spots:** Place potted plants near a sheltered wall or bring them into a greenhouse to protect roots from freezing.
- **Prune apples and pears:** Prune apple and pear trees while they are dormant, removing dead, damaged or overcrowded branches.
- **Harvest winter vegetables**: Pick hardy crops like kale, Brussels sprouts and leeks as needed, and clear any finished plants.
- **Clean greenhouses**: Wash greenhouse glass to maximize light and disinfect surfaces to remove less welcome creatures and diseases.
- **Check stored bulbs and tubers**: Inspect stored bulbs like dahlias and tubers for rot or shrivelling. Discard any damaged ones.
- **Order seeds for next year**: Browse catalogues and make your wish list for spring sowing to get ahead of the rush.
- **Plant tulips**: When the ground has frozen at least once, it is the best time to plant tulips.

Helleborus orientalis

LATE WINTER: GARDEN JOBS

- **Sow early seeds indoors:** Some seeds can be started as early as late winter. Hardy annuals like sweet peas, cobaea and broad beans can be started in pots in a greenhouse.
- **Prune wisteria**: Cut back summer growth to two or three buds from the main framework to encourage flowers.
- **Prune clematis**: If you're unsure which pruning group your clematis belongs to, observe when it flowers and use this simple rule:
    - *Flowers before early summer* (late spring to early summer): Do not prune. These clematis bloom on last year's growth and don't need cutting back.
    - *Pruning Group 1 (flowers from midsummer onwards)*: Prune in late winter. These varieties bloom on new growth and benefit from a yearly hard prune before spring growth begins.
    - *Pruning Group 2 (large-flowered clematis that bloom in midsummer on short stems that grew the previous year):* Remove any dead or weak stems in late winter to early spring.
    - *Pruning Group 3 (clematis that bloom from mid- to late summer, producing flowers on new growth from the current season):* In late winter–early spring, cut the plant back hard to the lowest pair of strong buds (about 30–60 cm/1–2 feet above the ground) to encourage fresh and vigorous growth.
- **Check stored bulbs and tubers**: Inspect stored dahlia tubers and other bulbs for rot or dehydration, and adjust storage conditions as needed.
- **Inspect and repair garden structures**: Fix broken fences, trellises or raised beds.
- **Plan your garden:** Sketch out planting plans, noting any changes or projects for the year ahead.
- **Force rhubarb**: Cover crowns with an upturned bucket to encourage early tender stems.
- **Prepare soil for planting in annual beds**: If cultivating flowers for cutting or vegetables for eating, you can remove last year's plant material from these beds and add well-rotted manure or compost to improve fertility and structure.
- **Check tools and equipment:** Sharpen blades, replace worn parts and stock up on essentials, such as twine or plant supports.
- **Chit seed potatoes:** Place seed potatoes in a cool, bright spot with the 'eyes' facing upwards to encourage sprouting.
- **Prune roses:** Choose a week that is not too cold to cut back hybrid teas and *Floribundas* to encourage strong growth and blooms in spring.
- **Sow sweet peas**: Best done in pots or modules under cover. Keep them in a cool, bright spot and pinch out the tips when they reach 10 cm (4 inches) tall to encourage bushier plants.
- **Cut back some herbaceous perennials**: Use secateurs to remove any herbaceous perennial stems that have turned mushy during the winter to prevent disease and to promote fresh spring growth. Add healthy material to your compost.

BASICS OF TOOL CARE

By dedicating a little time to tool care, you're investing in their longevity and performance. Plus, there's something uniquely rewarding about tending to the tools that help you tend to your garden. Sharp, clean tools help prevent the spread of disease among your plants and reduce unnecessary damage. They are safer and more effective, and they make every task feel a little more satisfying. Well-maintained tools can last a lifetime, even outliving us. In a world dominated by planned obsolescence, where so much is designed to be disposable, a little regular maintenance is an investment. I find that taking care of my tools and using them year after year can feel like its own kind of resistance to a throw-away world.

For best practice, wipe clean your tools at the end of use and store them in a dry place to prevent rust. A quick wipe with an oiled cloth before putting them away can make all the difference to their longevity. This guide is specifically written with secateurs in mind, but the key principles can be applied to sharpening and protecting hoes, trowels and hori horis. I sharpen my secateurs at least once a year, or when they start to rip stems instead of cleanly cut.

You will need:

- **Soapy water:** A bucket or spray bottle work well
- **Wire brush or stiff scrubbing brush:** If your tool is particularly dirty
- **Steel wool or a Clean Mate:** A scouring block for stubborn rust or sap
- **Clean cloths or rags:** For wiping down tools
- **Sharpening stone or diamond stone:** #1000 grit recommended for fine sharpening
- **Screwdriver or spanner:** Specific to your tools if you plan to disassemble
- **Camellia oil:** Or another rust-preventive oil
- **General-purpose tool lubricant:** For pivot points and moving parts; camellia oil can also be used
- **Protective gloves (optional):** Useful for handling sharp tools

1. CLEAN THE BLADES

Start by removing any dirt, sap or rust from the blades. Use soapy water and a wire brush or steel wool to tackle stubborn spots. For particularly tough grime, I swear by a Clean Mate – a small scouring block that works brilliantly to clean resin, rust and gunk off metal surfaces.

2. DISASSEMBLE FOR A THOROUGH CLEAN

Some brands of secateurs can be taken apart (they will usually be sent with instructions and a special tool for doing so). Some brands can't be taken apart as this would alter how they work. If you're cleaning secateurs that can be taken apart, disassemble them to access the blades more easily. Always follow the manufacturer's instructions to ensure safe and proper handling.

3. CHOOSE THE RIGHT SHARPENING STONE

For regular sharpening, a medium-grit sharpening stone or diamond stone works well. I recommend a #1000 grit for most sharpening jobs. Wet or oil the stone slightly, as per the manufacturer's guidance. My sharpening stone works best after soaking in water until the bubbles stop rising, which usually takes just a few minutes.

4. SHARPEN THE BLADES

Identify the bevelled edge of the blade – this is the angled edge that makes it sharp. Hold the stone at the same angle as the bevel and move it along the edge in a sweeping motion, always away from your body. Use consistent pressure and make long, even strokes. Repeat 5–10 times on one side. Feel the edge gently with your thumb or test by cutting a piece of paper. Always prioritize safety by handling tools carefully. If it's not sharp enough, repeat the process.

5. FINISH THE EDGE

For flat edges, use a finer grit stone to remove burrs by lightly dragging it across the blade's back.

6. REASSEMBLE AND PROTECT AGAINST RUST

Once sharpened, reassemble your tools if needed. Apply a few drops of camellia oil. This is excellent for protecting metal from rust. Use the Clean Mate to rub the oil into the blades, ensuring full coverage. Dry thoroughly before applying another layer of oil for added protection.

WATERING AND IRRIGATION

Watering is one of the simplest but most important ways we care for a garden. Young plants and anything in pots will always need extra attention, especially during dry spells or heatwaves when the soil can dry out quickly.

In a mild, temperate climate you may find that thoughtful planting; choosing the right plant for the right place (see page 75), together with a good layer of mulch means your garden holds onto moisture beautifully and needs very little watering, if any at all.

It helps to find a system that suits your life, whether that's keeping a watering can by the back door or setting up hoses and timers. Establishing a rhythm with watering saves time, effort, and water; particularly valuable if you're gardening in a hotter, drier climate.

BEST WATERING PRACTICES

Keeping your garden thriving starts with watering it the right way. Good watering habits, whether you're using a water butt and a watering can or a high-tech irrigation system, ensure your plants get the moisture they need at the right time of day to develop strong roots and stay healthy all season long.

Water in the morning and evening: The best times to water your garden are early in the morning and later in the evening. During these cooler parts of the day, less water is lost to evaporation, so your plants can absorb more moisture. Morning watering gets your plants ready to handle the day's heat, while evening watering keeps them hydrated through the night. If your nights tend to be cool and damp, it's usually best to water in the morning. It gives any splashed foliage time to dry in the sun, which helps keep fungal and pest problems at bay.

Water the soil, not the leaves of the plant: It's best to water the soil directly instead of sprinkling water on the leaves. When you water the soil, the moisture goes straight to the roots where it's most needed, promoting healthier and sturdier plant growth. Also, keeping the leaves dry helps prevent fungal diseases that can thrive in damp conditions. By focusing on the soil, you're giving your plants the best chance to grow well without the extra risk of leaf problems.

RAINWATER

The simplest way to water is by collecting rainwater in water butts or tubs connected to your gutters. Fill a watering can from the collected water as needed to water pots or easily accessible borders. This method is cost-effective, sustainable and works well for small gardens or a few containers.

While rainwater is an excellent resource for most garden plants, I avoid using collected rainwater for watering seedlings. Instead, I either place the seed trays outside to benefit directly from fresh rainfall or use mains water. This precaution is due to the potential for stagnant water in storage tanks to harbour harmful bacteria or pathogens that could negatively impact the delicate seedlings.

IRRIGATION SYSTEMS

For large gardens or areas with higher water needs, an irrigation system can make a world of difference. Drip irrigation, for example, is efficient and precise, delivering water directly to the soil and reducing waste. It's especially useful for potted gardens and flower beds where consistent moisture is critical.

It's best to have a monitored watering system so that you can tell how much water you are using. Paris and I do this by collecting rainwater in a tank and pumping from there. On the rare occasions that we need to add mains water to the tank, we can accurately measure exactly how much we're using so we can monitor our use of this precious resource.

HOW TO SET UP AN IRRIGATION SYSTEM

A durable drip irrigation line provides precise watering by releasing water at intervals directly into the soil. This minimizes waste and avoids wetting leaves, which can lead to sunburn or disease in humid conditions.

Opt for a tough, hard-wearing drip line, which looks like a hose, instead of flimsy drip tape, as we've found it lasts longer and requires far less maintenance. For cutting-garden beds, hoses with holes every 20 cm (8 inches) work well. For borders, a soaker hose might better suit your plants' water needs.

You will need:

- **Drip line irrigation:** Choose a durable drip line for beds, or a soaker hose for borders.
- **Connectors and fittings:** These connect hoses, tubing and emitters to create an irrigation network. Choose high-quality fittings to avoid leaks and ensure durability.
- **Access to water, be that from a tap, well, or a rainwater tank.**
- **Emitters or sprinkler heads:** Emitters can be attached to hoses at specific spots to send the water precisely to a particular plant or pot, while sprinklers work well for larger, open areas.
- **Pump:** If using a water tank or rainwater collection system, a pump will move the water from the tank into the irrigation pipes.

Optional parts for a timer system:

- **Solenoid and controller:** A solenoid valve automates water flow. Pairing it with a controller allows for scheduling, saving time and water. Modern controllers often include rainfall and moisture sensors, to adjust schedules based on real-time conditions.
- **Timer:** A timer allows you to automate watering schedules, ensuring your plants receive water at optimal times without manual intervention.

1. ASSESS YOUR GARDEN
Observe your garden layout, plant types and water needs. Identify areas that need watering and note whether certain plants require more or less water.

2. CHOOSE YOUR SYSTEM
Decide on an irrigation method.

- Drip line irrigation is best for large areas with evenly spaced plants.
- A hose with strategically placed emitter irrigation is precise and efficient, ideal for beds and pots.
- Sprinklers are good for lawns or wide-open spaces.
- Collect all necessary components for your specific needs, e.g. tubing, connectors, emitters, pump, solenoid, controller and timer. Be sure to choose materials suited to your chosen irrigation method.

3. INSTALL THE TUBING
Lay out the tubing along your garden beds or potted plants, connecting it to your water source. Follow manufacturer instructions for assembly.

4. POSITION THE IRRIGATION METHOD
Place emitters or sprinkler heads near the base of each plant to ensure even watering. Space them according to your plants' needs, i.e. close together for thirsty plants and farther apart for drought-tolerant ones. If you're planting evenly spaced plants, e.g. for a cut-flower garden, choose a drip line irrigation system with spacing that works for you.

5. TEST THE SYSTEM
Run water through the system to check for leaks and ensure even distribution. Adjust the water flow as needed and fix any issues before regular use.

6. ADD A TIMER OR CONTROLLER
Automate your watering schedule by adding a timer. For maximum efficiency, consider a controller with sensors that detect rainfall and soil moisture. This allows remote monitoring and ensures water is used only when necessary.

7. MONITOR AND ADJUST
Regularly check your system for blockages, leaks or uneven watering. Adjust as needed based on the season, weather and growth patterns of your plants.

COMPOST AND MULCH

Organic matter is the cornerstone of compost and mulch, essential for creating healthy soil. It consists mainly of plant materials, such as leaves, grass clippings and kitchen scraps, but also safe, animal-based by-products, such as manure, and shells. These materials naturally break down over time, releasing nutrients that enrich your soil and support plant growth.

MULCH

Mulch is any material used to cover the soil surface. It can be organic (such as compost, straw or bark) or inorganic (such as gravel or landscape fabric). Mulching is the act of spreading mulch over the soil surface to protect, enrich and improve it. This practice mimics nature's way of covering soil with fallen leaves and organic matter, providing a host of benefits, including:

Improvements to soil health: Organic mulch breaks down over time, enriching your soil with nutrients. It creates the perfect environment for earthworms and beneficial microbes.

Moisture rention: A layer of mulch reduces evaporation, helping your soil hold onto water.

Temperature regulation: Mulch protects your soil from temperature extremes, keeping it cool in the summer and insulated in the winter.

Improvements to soil structure and drainage: As mulch decomposes, it adds organic matter to the soil, improving its texture. Sandy soil becomes more loamy and moisture-retentive, while clay soil becomes more crumbly and better-draining. This enhances water movement through the soil, reducing pooling and waterlogging.

Weed suppression: A thick layer of mulch prevents sunlight from reaching weed seeds, inhibiting their growth.

Protection against erosion: Mulch shields the soil from heavy rain, strong winds and the baking sun.

WHAT TO LOOK FOR IN GOOD MULCHING COMPOST

Texture: The texture should be crumbly and able to retain moisture, not dusty or clumpy.

Quality: Organic green waste compost is ideal. Check for rubbish or contaminants.

Ingredients: If compost contains animal waste, ensure it's from animals fed on uncontaminated, unsprayed crops. This is to avoid compost with traces of aminopyralids, a pesticide that can harm certain plants, such as sweet peas, beans and tomatoes, isn't broken up by digestion in animals and can stay in the soil for up to six months. In wet climates, omit straw, as it can encourage slugs.

HOW TO MULCH

You can mulch at any time of year, but doing so in autumn and winter is ideal. This mimics nature, as fallen leaves naturally create a protective layer over the soil during these seasons.

1. CHOOSE YOUR MULCHING MATERIAL
Compost (see overleaf) is my favourite because it enriches the soil as it breaks down.

Avoid using materials such as wood chips for garden borders, as they can leach nutrients from the soil. However, I still utilize wood chips for some of the paths in my cut-flower cultivation areas, both in the garden and on the flower farm. I apply a thin layer of wood chips, ensuring they remain confined to the paths and do not scatter onto the growing beds. While wood chips can temporarily deplete soil nutrients as they break down, they ultimately replenish the soil once fully decomposed.

2. PREPARE YOUR BED
Remove perennial weeds and debris. If digging out weeds, disturb the soil structure as little as possible. Add weed roots and debris to your compost heap, but only if your heap gets hot enough to kill pathogens. If it doesn't, dispose of them separately.

3. SPREAD THE MULCH
Apply a 5–10-cm (2–4-inch) layer of mulch evenly across the bed, being careful not to pile it against plant stems or tree trunks, which can cause the plant to rot.

COMPOST

Compost is organic matter that has fully decomposed into a nutrient-rich material. In a way it's like a multivitamin for your soil, helping plants thrive by improving soil health, structure, and fertility.

Making your own compost is easier than you might think, and can be adapted to suit gardens of any size. There really are just four main ingredients required for successful composting: green nitrogen-rich material, brown carbon-rich material, oxygen and water.

It's a brilliant way to recycle kitchen scraps and garden waste, turning what might have gone in the bin into food for your plants. By composting, you cut down on waste going to landfill, reduce methane emissions, and need fewer chemical fertilizers. It's one of the simplest, most planet-friendly practices you can adopt in your garden. And it's genuinely satisfying to watch waste transform into something that gives back, closing the loop between kitchen, garden, and soil.

You will need:

- **Compost bin or heap:** See step 1 for advice on composting in small or large gardens
- **Balance of green and brown materials:**

Greens (nitrogen-rich): e.g. kitchen scraps, grass clippings, coffee grounds

Browns (carbon-rich): e.g. dry leaves, cardboard, straw

1. CHOOSING WHERE TO COMPOST

Small gardens: Use compact compost bins or tumblers that fit neatly into limited spaces. Chop large materials into smaller pieces to speed up decomposition. If space is extremely tight, consider community composting schemes, such as ShareWaste.

Large gardens: Build a multi-bay composting system. One bay can hold fresh material, another can decompose, and the third can store finished compost. To compost larger volumes of garden waste, such as pruned branches, use a chipper or shredder to break it down first.

2. HOW TO COMPOST

At first I aim for an approximate 50:50 split between layers of green materials and brown materials, then keep an eye on the mix in case it needs tweaking – too much green (nitrogen) turns the heap sludgy and smelly, while too much brown means the heap will take a really long time to decompose.

3. MOISTURE AND AIR FLOW

Keep your compost damp but not soggy. Turn it regularly to add oxygen and speed up decomposition. If you live in a very rainy area, you might need to add a lid to partially cover your compost heap.

LEAF MOULD

Leaf mould is a valuable soil amendment made from decomposed leaves. It's particularly easy to make and can greatly improve your garden's soil structure and moisture retention. Here's how to create your own leaf mould.

Collect fallen leaves: Shredding them with a mulching mower or running them through a shredder can speed up the process of making leaf mould, but this is an optional extra step.

Form a pile: Heap the leaves in a corner of your garden or another designated spot. You can leave the pile uncovered or use a simple wire frame to contain it.

Moisten and aerate: Keep the pile slightly moist by watering it occasionally. Turning the pile every few months can help aerate the leaves and speed up decomposition.

Wait: Allow the leaves to break down naturally over the course of 6–12 months. When the mould has a dark, crumbly texture and earthy smell, it's ready to use.

Put it to use: You can use your homemade leaf mould as a mulch, soil conditioner, or compost booster to enhance plant growth.

HOW TO DISPOSE OF DISEASED MATERIAL

Home composting: Suitable for plant material with less persistent infections. (*Note:* home compost bins rarely get hot enough to kill all pathogens.)

Green waste collection: Use your local council's service for infected material, as industrial composting reaches higher temperatures.

Burial: Bury infected leaves and fruit at least 30 cm (12 inches) deep in a designated, undisturbed spot, unless it's soil-borne or woody material.

Bonfires: Burn dry, woody material safely if permitted; follow local guidelines to avoid pollution and neighbour nuisance.

Household waste: As a last resort, dispose of small, infected prunings and seedlings in your general waste.

Council refuse site: For bulky or large woody debris not suitable for composting or burning, take it to your local tip.

DETERRING RATS

Whether you're in an urban or rural area, it's a good idea to secure your compost bin against rodents. These animals are attracted to food scraps and can be a nuisance regardless of your location, so using a sturdy lid and other rodent-proofing measures can help keep them away.

Choose a sturdy bin: Use a compost bin with a tightly fitting lid and solid sides.

Add a base: Place your bin on a layer of fine mesh or metal hardware cloth to prevent rodents from digging underneath.

Avoid food scraps that attract animals: Don't add meat, dairy or greasy food waste. I personally avoid throwing anything cooked in there too. Stick to fruit and vegetable scraps, coffee grounds and garden clippings.

Turn your compost regularly: Frequent turning disrupts rodents and speeds up decomposition.

Position wisely: Place the bin away from fences, walls or other structures that rodents could use for cover.

FEEDING YOUR GARDEN

If you're already composting and mulching to nourish your garden, there are additional organic methods you can use to further enhance soil fertility and support healthy plant growth. These approaches complement your composting and mulching efforts, targeting specific plant needs and soil conditions.

Apply organic feeds during the growing season when plants are actively taking up nutrients. You can foliar feed (spray the leaves), or work feed into the soil. Use a soil test (see page 23) to identify deficiencies and tailor feeding to your garden's specific needs. Begin with light applications to avoid overfeeding, which can harm plants and the environment.

ORGANIC LIQUID FEEDS

Comfrey tea: High in potassium, ideal for flowering and fruiting plants.

Nettle tea: Rich in nitrogen, perfect for leafy greens and young plants.

To make your own feed, steep your chosen leaves in water for 1–2 weeks, then strain. Dilute (1 part liquid feed to 10 parts water) and apply at the base of plants or as a foliar spray. We do this weekly (when we remember!) or when the plants look like they're in need of a boost.

GREEN MANURES

Plants such as clover, alfalfa and mustard can be grown as a green manure crop (or cover crop) to enrich the soil, helping to fix nitrogen, improve soil fertility, suppress weeds and prevent erosion.

Sow in empty garden beds after harvesting. Once established, cut down before flowering and dig into the soil to decompose.

Phacelia, shown on the right, is often used as a green manure, dug into the soil to boost nutrients and improve structure before planting. It's also a favourite of pollinators and makes a lovely, long-lasting cut flower, which makes me love it even more.

BONE MEAL AND BLOOD MEAL

Bone meal: High in phosphorus, supports root development and flowering.

Blood meal: High in nitrogen, encourages leafy growth.

Sprinkle the meal lightly around plants, or mix into the soil, following the package instructions. Great for bulbs, vegetables and perennials.

SEAWEED AND KELP PRODUCTS

Fertilizers derived from seaweed are rich in trace minerals and natural growth stimulants, which can strengthen plant resistance to unwelcome creatures and diseases, as well as promoting vigorous root growth and overall health.

Apply as a liquid feed, or mix granular seaweed products into the soil, following product instructions.

WORM CASTINGS

Also known as vermicompost, these are nutrient-rich by-products of composting worms that contain balanced nutrients and promote beneficial microbial activity.

You can obtain worm castings from your garden if it has an active population of earthworms (you can sometimes spot them in lawns). As they move through the soil and process organic matter, earthworms naturally produce castings that enrich your garden soil. However, if you want a more concentrated or easily harvestable source of worm castings, setting up a dedicated wormery (vermicompost system) is often more effective.

Add a handful to planting holes or use as a top-dressing around plants. Especially effective for container gardens and seedlings.

AGED MANURE

This is animal manure (cow, horse or chicken) that has been aged or composted to prevent burning plants. It can add nitrogen, phosphorus and potassium to the soil. Be wary of aminopyralids – you need to be sure the animals are feeding from fields and hay that have not been sprayed with chemicals and weed killers.

Apply as a top-dressing around plants or mix into the soil during preparation. Avoid using fresh manure.

Above: Phacelia, a green manure and great cut flower, in full flower

PRUNING

Shaping, strengthening, and encouraging growth

Rose 'The Ancient Mariner'

My grandmother, GJ – whose poem about her father, another keen gardener, opens this book – was the one who first taught me how to prune. At the time it felt confusing, almost too technical, and I remember worrying I'd do more harm than good. But over the years I've learned to see it differently; pruning is a moment to pause, slow down, and really connect with a plant. Once you get the feel for it, it's as satisfying as giving a shrub a good haircut.

Every tree, rose, and shrub responds a little differently, so notice how each one grows back and let that shape your approach next time. To begin with, go gently. Take a little less than you think you need to, you can always cut more later, but you can't stick a branch back on. With time, you'll fall into the rhythm of each plant and pruning will become second nature. And don't worry, most plants, especially roses, can take a good cut back and will come back healthier, happier, and more generous for it.

PRUNING ROSES

My middle name is Róża, Polish for Rose – a name passed down from my great-aunt on my father's side. My great-great-grandmother must have loved roses enough to name her daughter Róża, and in that ancestral thread, I like to think I'm tangibly tracing back my family's long-held love for them.

My birthday falls right in the heart of rose season, making their blooms even more special to me. Every year, someone will undoubtedly give me a rose as a gift to add my collection, knowing that no other present brings me greater joy. There are over 150 roses in my garden now, each one associated with the loved one who gave it to me and a memory of them. As they flower again each year, I feel a deep sense of gratitude for the love they represent, their beauty carrying so much meaning and connection. For all these reasons, roses remain my favourite flower – in the wild, the garden and the vase.

Roses carry a reputation for being fussy and difficult, but in truth, they're far more forgiving than many people think. They are surprisingly robust and adaptable, making them a joy to grow in almost any garden. They thrive with just a few basic care principles and will reward even the smallest effort with blooms that are second to none. Even if you make a mistake, or need to prune them right back, they'll often respond with more vigorous growth and abundant flowers; they are, in their very fibre, such resilient plants. Many varieties are drought-tolerant once established, and they're happier in less-than-perfect soil than their reputation suggests. There's a rose for every situation: climbing roses to drape over arches or walls, bush roses for structured beds, and wild species roses that bring a natural feel to your garden while supporting wildlife with their hips.

WHY WE PRUNE ROSES

Pruning roses is essential for their health, vigour and aesthetic appeal. It encourages new growth, improves air circulation, prevents disease and promotes more abundant blooms. Pruning also helps shape the rose, keeping it manageable and ensuring it remains a focal point in the garden. While it may feel daunting at first, pruning roses is a straightforward process once you understand a few key principles.

The timing of rose pruning depends on the type of rose and your climate.

Winter pruning: In most regions, the best time to prune roses is in late winter or early spring, just as buds begin to swell, before new growth fully emerges.

Summer pruning (deadheading): During the growing season, you can deadhead roses by removing spent blooms to encourage repeat flowering. I still cut deep into the plant when deadheading. This encourages the next set of shoots to grow long and strong.

Rose 'Port Sunlight' and white foxgloves (*Digitalis purpurea albaflora*)

HOW TO PRUNE ROSES

1. START WITH CLEAN, SHARP TOOLS

Use sharp secateurs to make clean cuts. Clean and sterilize your tools with rubbing alcohol to prevent the spread of disease (see page 196).

2. REMOVE DEAD, DISEASED OR DAMAGED WOOD

Start by cutting out any dead, blackened or broken stems. Cut back to healthy wood, which is green just beneath the bark.

3. THIN OUT CROWDED GROWTH

Remove weak or spindly stems and any that cross or rub against each other. This improves air circulation and reduces the risk of fungal diseases.

4. SHAPE THE PLANT

Aim for an open, vase-like shape with stems fanning outwards. This allows sunlight to penetrate the centre of the plant and also permits good air flow, which can help prevent diseases from settling on the plant.

5. CUT ABOVE OUTWARD-FACING BUDS

Make cuts at a 45-degree angle about 5 mm (¼ inch) above a healthy, outward-facing bud. The direction the bud is pointing is the direction it will grow in. Cutting an outward-facing bud encourages the plant to grow outwards, not inwards.

6. TRIM TO THE DESIRED HEIGHT

For hybrid teas and *Floribundas*, cut stems down to 30–45 cm (12–18 inches) or to approximately one-third of their mature height. For shrub roses, a lighter prune to maintain shape and size is often sufficient.

7. DISPOSE OF CLIPPINGS

Remove all pruned material from around the plant to prevent the spread of disease.

PRUNING FRUIT TREES

Out of all the plants I grow, it's the apple trees that really set the rhythm of the year. My husband Ted makes cider from the fruit; it's a joyful way to preserve the yields of the season.

From winter pruning to autumn harvest, the year turns on their needs: pruning in the cold months, protecting blossom from frost, thinning fruit in summer, and pressing apples in autumn. We seek out old Sussex varieties, often with their names long lost, grafting them to vigorous rootstock to keep their history alive.

WHY WE PRUNE FRUIT TREES

While there are many shapes into which you can train your tree, the most popular is what is referred to as the open goblet. This shape promotes good air flow as well as access to light, both of which are essential for a healthy tree and ripe fruit. If you have a young tree, wait a few years for it to establish before cutting the central leader stem, leaving the lateral branches to form the goblet shape. We love the old saying 'You should be able to throw your cap through a well-pruned apple tree'. In fact, it is good advice for most fruit trees.

Pruning fruit trees helps maintain their structure, encourages healthy growth and increases fruit production. By opening up the canopy, pruning allows sunlight to reach the inner branches and improves air flow, reducing the risk of disease. It also helps manage the tree's size, making it easier to harvest fruit.

ENCOURAGING ANNUAL FRUITING

Apple trees are naturally biennial, meaning that they tend to produce a heavy crop every other year. However, you can encourage more consistent yearly fruiting by balancing the vegetative growth and reducing the amount of unproductive wood. By focusing the tree's energy on fruit production, you'll achieve a healthier, more balanced harvest year to year.

WHEN TO PRUNE FRUIT TREES

Winter pruning: Most fruit trees, including apples and pears, are pruned in late winter, when the tree is dormant. This encourages vigorous growth in spring and allows for better visibility of the tree's structure. Winter is the ideal time to establish or refine the tree's shape.

Summer pruning: Stone fruits, such as cherries and plums, are best pruned in midsummer to reduce the risk of diseases such as silver leaf. Summer pruning is used to control size, thin out excessive growth and improve fruit quality by redirecting energy to ripening fruit.

HOW TO PRUNE FRUIT TREES

1. ASSESS THE TREE
Before starting to prune, step back and evaluate the tree's overall shape. Look for dead, diseased or overcrowded branches that need removing.

2. START WITH DEAD, DISEASED OR DAMAGED WOOD
Cut out any branches that are dead, infected or broken. Make cuts back to healthy wood or to the trunk.

3. REMOVE SUCKERS AND WATERSPROUTS
Suckers (shoots growing from the base) and water shoots (vertical shoots growing from branches) sap energy from the tree and should be removed.

4. SHAPE FOR THE TREES PURPOSE
For open-centre (goblet shaped) trees: Once they are a few years old, remove the central leader and keep 5–7 strong, outward-reaching scaffold branches.

For central leader trees (apples, pears where livestock graze beneath): Keep the main vertical stem and remove competing uprights.

5. THIN OUT THE CANOPY
Prune branches that cross, rub or grow inwards. This allows sunlight to penetrate the tree's centre and encourages good air flow to prevent disease.

6. SHORTEN LONG BRANCHES AND MANAGE VERTICAL SHOOTS
Cut back to 2–3 buds during the dormant season, choosing a bud facing in the direction you want the branch to grow; the future is decided here. Cut just above a bud.

7. ENCOURAGE SPUR FORMATION
On apple and pear trees, leave short, stubby growths (spurs). Most apple and pear trees produce fruit on spurs, which are shoots that sprout off older wood.

PRUNING SHRUBS

Pruning shrubs is one of those tasks that can feel intimidating if you're new to gardening, but it's much simpler than it seems and so rewarding for many reasons. Removing dead, damaged or diseased branches helps the shrub focus its energy where it's needed most. Pruning can keep shrubs looking the shape and size you want and can prevent them from getting leggy or overgrown. Thinning out dense growth reduces unwanted creatures and diseases while letting light reach all parts of the plant, and many shrubs produce more blooms or fruit after a good prune; I like to think of it as their way of saying thank you!

WHEN TO PRUNE SHRUBS

The timing depends on the type of shrub and how it grows.

Spring-flowering shrubs: Prune after they bloom because they form buds on last year's growth. If you prune too early, you might accidentally cut off next year's flowers. **Examples:** forsythia, lilac, flowering quince

Summer-flowering shrubs: Prune in late winter or early spring before new growth begins. These plants bloom on the current year's growth, so pruning now encourages fresh flowers. **Examples:** butterfly bush, *Hydrangea paniculata*, rose of Sharon

Evergreen shrubs: Lightly prune in late spring or early summer to keep their shape. **Examples:** boxwood, holly, yew

Deciduous shrubs: Prune during dormancy in late winter or early spring to help them bounce back strongly in the growing season. **Examples:** spiraea, dogwood

TECHNIQUES TO TRY

Deadheading: Snip off spent flowers to tidy up and encourage more blooms (great for hydrangeas and roses).

Heading back: Trim back branches to control the size or encourage bushier growth. This technique focuses on reducing the length of a branch while leaving the rest of the shrub intact. To head back a branch, identify a healthy bud or lateral branch that is pointing in the direction you want new growth to go (ideally outwards rather than inwards). Make your cut just above this bud or branch. Heading back on hydrangeas or roses like this, usually about a third of the plant, will result in more flowers, but usually smaller and on less strong stems.

Thinning out: Remove entire stems from the base, whether that's where it meets the main stem or branches out from the ground. This promotes a better air flow and a more natural look.

Rejuvenation pruning: For older, overgrown shrubs, cut back one-third of the oldest stems each year over three years. This gradual process avoids shocking the plant and keeps it looking great. For roses and hydrangeas, I cut down two-thirds of the plant's mature size each year. I find this gives me stronger stems and better-quality flowers.

HOW TO PRUNE SHRUBS

1. PREPARE YOUR TOOLS
Start with sharp, clean secateurs or loppers for small branches, and a pruning saw for anything thicker. Clean and sterilize your tools (see page 196 or 218) between cuts, especially if dealing with diseased material, to avoid spreading issues.

2. START WITH THE BASICS
Remove dead, damaged or diseased wood first. Cut out any branches that cross or rub against each other to prevent damage.

3. SHAPE THE SHRUB
For a natural look, prune lightly, following the shrub's natural growth pattern. For a more formal look, trim evenly to create a neat, structured shape.

4. THINNING OUT
Remove some of the oldest, woodiest stems at the base to let light and air into the centre. This encourages fresh growth and helps the shrub stay vigorous.

5. MAKE CLEAN CUTS
Always cut just above a bud that faces outwards. This encourages new growth to spread away from the centre, keeping the shrub open and airy. Make cuts at an angle to prevent water from pooling on the cut surface.

CUTTING BACK AND CLEARING

Cutting back plants helps prepare your garden for the next growing season. It encourages healthy growth by redirecting the plant's energy, and creates a neat, organized appearance in spring. Plus, it gives you a chance to take stock of your garden, make notes about what worked well and enjoy the satisfaction of a seasonal reset.

WHEN TO DO IT

Many people cut back before winter, but increasingly gardeners are leaving the borders standing until spring. For herbaceous perennials, you can cut them back in late autumn if you prefer a tidy winter look. But there is good reason to leave them standing until early spring, and that is to enjoy their seed heads sparkling with frost and to provide food and shelter for wildlife, such as birds and insects. Air pockets are trapped between the stems and leaves and act as a protective barrier of the plant's crowns from extreme cold for the more cold-sensitive plants, such as gaura and *Salvia* 'Amistad'. On top of the habitat it creates, it also can look beautiful!

The seed heads of phlomis, foxgloves, sea holly, asters, *Allium nigrum*, rudbeckia, honesty, sedum, achillea and sidalcea are some of my favourites to keep around through winter. Their silhouettes can look particularly beautiful on a frosty day.

HOW TO DO IT

Start with sharp, clean secateurs or shears to make clean cuts, reducing the risk of introducing disease. For herbaceous perennials, trim dead, mushy or fallen stems down to ground level. For shrubs, prune selectively based on their specific needs, removing dead, damaged or overcrowded branches to maintain their shape and health. Remove all debris as you go, you can use a trug or a wheelbarrow for ease, and add healthy material to your compost pile.

CARING FOR PLANTS IN POTS

Pots have limited soil, which means nutrients and water are used up more quickly than in the ground. Without regular care, potted plants can become stressed and fail to thrive. By watering, feeding and repotting as needed, you're ensuring your plants have the best chance to grow, bloom and bring beauty to your space.

WHEN TO DO IT

Caring for potted plants is a year-round task, but certain times of the year call for extra attention. During hot, dry months, pots can dry out quickly, so you'll need to monitor their moisture levels closely. In winter, tender plants are vulnerable to frost and need protection from freezing temperatures. Regularly checking your pots throughout the year ensures your plants stay happy and healthy.

HOW TO DO IT

Watering: Check the top 2.5 cm (1 inch) of soil – if it feels dry, it's time to water. Water thoroughly, allowing it to drain through the bottom of the pot to prevent waterlogging. Be consistent but mindful of overwatering, especially during cooler months.

Feeding: Potted plants rely entirely on you for nutrients, so feed them regularly with an appropriate fertilizer during the growing season. Use a liquid feed (see page 204) for quick results, or slow-release granules for a steady supply of nutrients. Tailor the fertilizer to the plant's needs (e.g. high-potash feed for flowering plants, and nitrogen-rich feed for leafy greens).

Repotting: Every 1–2 years, refresh the compost to replenish nutrients and give the roots space to grow. Move the plant to a slightly larger pot if it has outgrown its current one, or prune the roots if you want to maintain its size.

Winter care: Be sure to raise your pots up on 'feet' (bricks or pieces of broken pots) for overwintering, as this allows excess rain to drain properly and prevents water pooling around the roots, which can lead to root rot in colder months. Elevating pots also improves air circulation around them, reducing the risk of frost damage and helping the soil to stay drier and healthier. For tender plants, move pots to a sheltered spot, such as a greenhouse, porch or sunny windowsill indoors. If that's not possible, you can wrap pots with insulating materials, such as horticultural fleece or bubble wrap to protect the roots.

WEEDING

Clearing space for what you want to thrive

There is so much to share on the topic of weeding. Weeding is fairly essential for giving your plants the best chance to thrive, as the weeds compete for water, nutrients and sunlight, often crowding out your chosen plants. There's no arguing that regular weeding keeps your garden looking neat and cared for and reduces habitats for less welcome wildlife (especially slugs who thrive with extra vegetative protection). It can even be meditative, helping you connect with your garden's rhythms and needs. But let's be honest: it can also feel like an overwhelming task that puts you off gardening entirely.

Weeding is more subjective than it might seem. One person's weed can be another person's wild flower, and the line between the two is often blurred. Who decides what counts as a weed and what deserves a place in the garden? Take dandelions: often dismissed as a nuisance, these cheerful flowers are a vital early-season food source for pollinators such as bees and butterflies. Nettles, while unwelcome in many borders, support several butterfly species, including the red admiral and peacock, making them invaluable in their wildlife support.

Historically, many plants we now call weeds were once prized for their usefulness. Chickweed, for example, can be eaten as a nutritious green, while comfrey has long been used to heal wounds and to make plant fertilizer. Even bindweed, notorious for its invasive tendencies and a personal gardening nemesis of mine, produces delicate, trumpet-shaped flowers that attract pollinators. In fact, the first flower I remember being given as a child was a bindweed bloom, plucked by my father and gifted to me as my own special treasure. That small act turned something that is often maligned into a cherished memory.

Ultimately, weeding is about finding a balance between aesthetics, practicality and personal preference. By understanding the ecological value of these so-called weeds, you can decide where they belong – or don't – in your garden. Perhaps you'll find that a few are worth keeping, not just for the wildlife they support, but for the stories they tell and the beauty they can bring when seen in a different light.

WHEN TO DO IT

Weeding is a task best done little and often, particularly during the growing season when weeds can spread rapidly. Start early in spring to catch weeds before they flower and set seed, and continue through summer and autumn. Weeding after a good rain is ideal because wet soil makes it easier to remove the roots.

HOW TO DO IT

Begin by identifying the weeds in your garden (a quick search in a plant encyclopedia or app can help with unfamiliar ones). For small or shallow-rooted weeds, pull them out by hand, grasping as close to the root as possible to avoid breakage, this is the method I use to deal with my perennial bindweed problem.

A hoe is a fantastic tool for slicing off weeds at the surface, particularly in vegetable beds or borders. Once you've cleared an area, apply a layer of mulch (see page 201) to suppress weed growth and retain soil moisture. For persistent weeds pathways or patios, consider natural remedies, such as pouring boiling water or a vinegar solution, over the area and scrubbing it off.

GLOSSARY AND IDENTIFICATION OF 10 COMMON GARDEN WEEDS

1. **Bindweed** *Convolvulus arvensis*: Twining vine with white or pink trumpet-shaped flowers.
2. **Chickweed** *Stellaria media*: Low-growing with small white flowers.
3. **Couch grass** *Elymus repens*: Spreading grass with underground rhizomes.
4. **Creeping buttercup** *Ranunculus repens*: Low-growing with runners of leaves with small yellow flowers.
5. **Dandelion** *Taraxacum officinale*: Bright yellow flowers; deep taproot.
6. **Dock** *Rumex obtusifolius*: Large, red-veined leaves; deep roots; its tall spikes of small greenish flowers turn reddish-brown as they mature.
7. **Ground elder** *Aegopodium podagraria*: Spreading clumps of light green, serrated leaves and white umbellifer flowers.
8. **Mare's tail** *Equisetum arvense*: Thin, spiky shoots resembling a horse's tail.
9. **Nettle** *Urtica dioica*: Jagged leaves; stings on contact.
10. **Shepherd's purse** *Capsella bursa-pastoris*: Small white flowers and heart-shaped seed pods.

LESS WELCOME CREATURES AND DISEASES

You may have noticed by now that I prefer the term 'less welcome creatures' to pests! Monitoring and keeping less welcome creatures and diseases in check is an ongoing part of gardening. By observing your plants regularly and taking action early, you can prevent small issues from becoming major problems. Plus, there are many natural and organic ways to address these challenges while keeping your garden thriving and wildlife-friendly.

For general prevention, clean and disinfect tools regularly, especially after pruning diseased plants. Mulch around plants to retain soil moisture and regulate temperature.

To identify the issue, use gardening books, reliable websites or plant identification apps to confirm what's affecting your plant. Accurate identification is key to effective treatment – less welcome creatures and diseases each require different approaches.

DEALING WITH LESS WELCOME CREATURES

Hand-pick large less welcome creatures: Remove visible caterpillars, beetles or slugs by hand. If you can face it, drop them into a bucket of soapy water to prevent them from returning.

Encourage natural predators: Invite beneficial insects, such as ladybirds, lacewings and parasitic wasps, into your garden. You can do this by planting flowers such as marigolds, yarrow (achillea) and cosmos.

Organic solutions: Try nematodes (parasitic worms that feed on specific creatures, such as slugs) or homemade sprays (e.g. garlic and chilli spray) to deter less welcome creatures. Always test on a small area first to ensure it doesn't harm your plants.

Companion planting: Grow plants strategically together to naturally deter less welcome creatures. Here are some classic combinations:

- **Marigolds:** Repel aphids, nematodes and whiteflies.
- **Basil:** Protects tomatoes by repelling flies and mosquitoes.
- **Onions and garlic:** Keep carrot flies, aphids and slugs at bay.
- ***Nasturtiums*:** Draw aphids and cabbage worms away from more vulnerable crops e.g. kale and broccoli.

DEALING WITH DISEASES

Remove affected parts: Cut off infected leaves, stems or flowers and dispose of them. Sometimes it's a case of removing the plant in its entirety. If your compost heap does not get really hot, do not add infected plants as they may spread the disease. You can check the temperature with a compost thermometer – you need a minimum reading of at least 55°C (131°F) for at least three days in a row. Temperatures of 54–57°C (130–135°F) are usually enough to kill most pathogens, fly larvae and weed seeds.

Improve air flow: Thin out dense foliage to improve ventilation and reduce humidity, which can encourage fungal diseases such as powdery mildew and blight.

Avoid overhead watering: Wet foliage is a breeding ground for fungal infections. Instead, water at the base of the plant to keep leaves dry.

Boost plant immunity: Use compost tea – a solution made by steeping finished compost in water, often with added ingredients, such as seaweed extract. This process extracts beneficial microbes, nutrients and organic compounds from the compost into the water. When applied to plants as a foliar spray or soil drench, compost tea can help strengthen plant immunity, improve nutrient uptake and support overall plant health, making plants more resistant to diseases. Seaweed-based fertilizers work similarly by providing a natural source of trace minerals and growth hormones that enhance plant resilience.

10 COMMON LESS WELCOME GARDEN CREATURES AND DISEASES

Aphids: Tiny green, black or white sap-sucking insects that cluster on new growth.

Black spot (on roses): Black circular spots on yellowing leaves; often causes leaves to drop prematurely.

Blight (on tomatoes/potatoes): Rapid blackening of stems, leaves and fruits or tubers, leading to rot.

Box tree moth: Larvae (caterpillars) chew through box leaves, leaving skeletonized foliage and webbing. Droppings (frass) are often found around damaged areas.

Powdery mildew: White, powdery fungal coating on leaves, stems and flowers.

Red spider mites: Tiny creatures that create fine webbing; leaves may appear mottled or stippled.

Rust: Orange, yellow or brown pustules on leaf undersides, causing distortion and defoliation.

Slugs and snails: Leave mucus trails and chew irregular holes in leaves, especially on young plants.

Spider mites: Tiny creatures that create fine webbing; leaves may appear mottled or stippled.

Vine weevils: Larvae feed on roots, causing plants to wilt; adults chew distinctive notches in leaf edges.

Whitefly: Tiny white insects that fly up in clouds when disturbed, often found on the undersides of leaves.

LAWN MAINTENANCE

Lawn maintenance isn't my favourite garden task, but with pets, a toddler and a penchant for hosting summer picnics with friends and family, my lawn sees plenty of use. Fortunately, maintaining a healthy lawn doesn't have to rely on chemical fertilizers and pesticides. Organic practices reduce the run-off of harmful chemicals into waterways, preserving local water quality and aquatic life, while a wildlife-friendly lawn provides habitat and food sources for beneficial insects, birds and other wildlife, promoting a balanced ecosystem.

SPRING

Raking: Gently rake the grass with a spring-tined rake, taking care not to tear it. This removes winter debris and lifts grass and weed foliage for more efficient cutting. Leave a pile to one side for birds to use in building their nests.

Sowing bare patches: Once the soil warms, sow bare patches by forking the soil to break it up, then firming and levelling it before applying appropriate grass seed. Cover the seeded areas with fleece to keep birds off, and water regularly. Introduce native grasses and wild flowers to provide food and habitat for local wildlife.

First mowing: Your first cut of the season should not be too short, especially if a sunny day is followed by a nighttime frost. Leaving the grass slightly longer helps protect it from sudden temperature drops.

SUMMER

Regular mowing: Focus on maintaining your lawn through regular mowing. Hand-dig weeds, especially prickly ones, such as thistles, or leave them in place, allowing a biodiverse range of plants to grow in your lawn.

Mowing practices: Keep your grass trimmed to about 8 cm (3 inches) tall, to ensure the soil stays shaded, to minimize weed proliferation and to create a habitat for insects. When conditions become dry and grass growth slows, reduce the frequency of mowing and further increase the cutting height to allow the blades to grow longer. This practice encourages the development of deeper roots, enhancing the lawn's resilience. Cutting the grass too short during dry spells can weaken it, making it more prone to damage and stress. In an ideal world, once your lawn is established, don't water it, as water is such a precious resource. Rely on rainfall instead, which encourages the grass roots to grow deep to search out water for themselves. This helps a lawn to become more self-reliant in the long run.

Compost grass clippings, especially if you have clover growing among the grass. Make sure to balance your compost pile with brown ingredients, as grass clippings are high in nitrogen (see page 202).

No-mow May: In the UK, No-mow May is a dedicated period when gardeners are encouraged to refrain from mowing their lawns. This initiative supports pollinators, such as bees and butterflies, by allowing wild flowers and grasses to bloom undisturbed. By not mowing, you provide essential nectar sources and habitat for these beneficial insects during a critical time in their lifecycle.

Encourage natural diversity: Leave some areas uncut to create an interesting mix of order and adventure. Plant or sow flowers within the long grass to attract pollinating insects (see page 174 on establishing a wildflower meadow). Even in small, urban gardens, the introduction of a wildflower meadow strip in a lawn can be naturally beautiful.

AUTUMN

This optional, but lots of people do this practise. Aerate the soil to improve nutrient and water penetration. You can do this by pushing a garden fork in to a depth of 7.5 cm (3 inches) to make holes at intervals. This helps the lawn recover from the summer heat and prepares it for the cooler months ahead.

WINTER

In wet areas, minimize foot traffic to protect the grass from damage.

GLOSSARY OF TERMS

Aminopyralid: A group of herbicides used to control broadleaf weeds, often found in agricultural or pasture settings; if an animal eats crops sprayed with them, they pass into its dropping. They persist in manure and compost for 6–12 months, potentially harming sensitive plants if they are used in gardens.

Basal: Referring to the base of a plant, where stems or shoots emerge near ground level. Basal shoots are new growth sprouting from the base of a plant.

Bed/border: Designated areas in the garden where plants are grown, often framed by paths, walls or lawns. Beds are typically viewed from all sides, while borders are viewed from one side.

Cloche: A small, dome-shaped cover, traditionally made of glass or plastic, used to protect individual plants from frost, pests and harsh weather. Its design allows sunlight to pass through while retaining heat around the plant.

Cold frame: A low, transparent structure that sits directly on the ground to protect plants from cold weather. It creates a warm microclimate, extending the growing season by trapping solar heat and shielding plants from frost.

Cold stratification: The process of exposing seeds to a period of cold and moisture to mimic winter conditions, which triggers them to germinate once temperatures rise.

Compaction: What happens when soil gets squashed – whether by heavy feet or machinery. Compacted soil stops to let water, air and roots moving freely, making it tough for plants to grow.

Coppicing: A pruning technique that involves cutting trees or shrubs to ground level, which causes new shoots to grow from the base. Coppiced trees are often multi-stemmed and have a lower canopy height than average.

Cut-and-come-again: These are plants that can be repeatedly harvested for their blooms throughout the growing season without harming the plant. This allows gardeners to enjoy continuous flowers by regularly cutting stems while promoting further flowering. **Examples:** sweet peas, cosmos, dahlias.

Cutting: A small snippet of a plant – stem, leaf or root – used to grow a brand-new one. It's one of the easiest and most rewarding ways to multiply your favourite plants.

Deadheading: The process of removing spent flowers from a plant to encourage new blooms and prevent the plant from going to seed which prolongs the season of flowering.

Dormancy: A resting stage for seeds or plants, often occurring during cold or dry seasons. During this period, growth slows or stops entirely, allowing the plant or seed to conserve energy until conditions improve.

Ericaceous: Refers to plants that thrive in acidic soil with a pH level below 7, typically requiring well-drained, nutrient-rich conditions free from lime. **Examples:** rhododendrons, azaleas, blueberries.

Evergreen: Plants that keep their leaves through every season, even in the depths of winter; perfect for adding structure and a sense of permanence to your space. **Examples:** holly, boxwood, pine tree.

Germination: The process by which a seed begins to grow and develop into a seedling. This happens when the seed absorbs water, swells and breaks through its outer shell. With the right combination of moisture, warmth and sometimes light, the seedling emerges, starting the plant's life cycle.

Hardening off: The process of gradually acclimatizing seedlings or young plants grown indoors to outdoor conditions before planting them in the garden. This prevents shock and helps them adjust to changes in temperature, light and wind.

Hardscaping: The non-living elements of a garden, such as paths, walls, patios and fences, which provide structure and define spaces.

Herbaceous: Soft-stemmed plants that die back completely in winter, retreating underground, only to burst forth again in spring. **Examples:** delphiniums, peonies.

Hummocks: Small, rounded mounds of earth or vegetation, often formed naturally in wetlands, meadows, or forested areas.

In the green: Refers to actively growing plants, that are still in leaf. The best stage to transplant certain plants (often bulbs). **Example:** snowdrops.

Invasive species: Non-native plants that spread aggressively, competing with native vegetation and disrupting ecosystems.

Mulch: A layer of material (such as bark, straw, compost or gravel) spread over the soil surface to retain moisture, suppress weeds and regulate soil temperature.

Native plants: Plants that have evolved and occur naturally in a specific region or ecosystem, thriving without human intervention and supporting local wildlife.

Nematodes: Microscopic worms that can be watered into the soil as a natural pest control; certain types can seek out and kill slugs, helping to protect young plants without the need for chemicals.

Nodes: The little bumps or joints on a stem where leaves, branches or flowers emerge. They're also where new growth happens if you take a cutting.

Overwinter: The process of helping plants survive through the winter, whether by protecting them outdoors or bringing them indoors to avoid frost damage.

Plant reversion: The phenomenon where a cultivated plant unexpectedly reverts to its original, wild traits, often losing desired characteristics, such as colour or size.

Propagation: The creation of new plants, whether by sowing seeds, taking cuttings, or dividing existing ones. It's a fun and thrifty way to expand your garden.

Root: The underground part of a plant that anchors it in the soil, absorbs water and nutrients, and stores energy.

Runners: Long, horizontal stems that grow above or below the ground, producing new plants at their tips. **Examples:** strawberries, mint, crocosmia.

Saplings: Small, immature trees that are past the seedling stage but not yet fully grown, often characterized by thin, flexible trunks.

Seedlings: Young plants that have recently germinated from seeds, typically with just their first set of leaves (cotyledons) or a few true leaves (the same leaves they will have when they reach maturity).

Self-seeders: Plants that naturally drop their seeds at the end of their growing season. These seeds germinate on their own, often in the same location or nearby, creating new plants without any intervention. Self-seeders can give your garden a charming, spontaneous look and help fill gaps in borders. **Examples:** poppies, calendula, nigella, aquilegia, verbena.

Shoots: New growth on a plant, including stems, leaves and buds.

Softscaping: All the plants, trees and flowers that bring colour, texture and life to your space.

Stem: The main support structure of a plant, connecting roots to leaves and flowers, and transporting water and nutrients.

Taproot: The primary, central root of a plant that grows straight down, anchoring the plant and storing nutrients. **Examples:** docks, dandelions, carrots.

The right plant for the right place: A principle of gardening that involves selecting plants suited to your garden's specific conditions, such as soil type, light levels and climate, for healthier growth and less maintenance.

Threshing: The process of separating seeds from stalks and seed heads, typically by beating or crushing the harvested plant material.

Umbellifer: Umbrella-like clusters of flowers, often flat-topped and great for pollinators. **Examples:** dill, fennel, cow parsley.

Under cover: In gardening, under cover means growing plants in a protected environment, such as a greenhouse, polytunnel, cold frame, or indoors. This helps shield plants from frost, less welcome creatures, and harsh weather while providing warmth and extending the growing season. It's especially useful for starting seeds early, protecting tender plants or creating ideal conditions for growth.

Vermiculite: A lightweight mineral that retains water and keeps soil airy, helping seeds to stay moist for germination.

Vernalisation: The requirement for some plants to experience a spell of cold before they can flower, ensuring blooms occur in the right season.

Whip: A young, slender, unbranched tree, typically 2–4 years old, sold for planting. Whips establish quickly, adapt well to their environment, and are often preferred for long-term growth over more mature, expensive trees. While they may take longer to develop into fully structured trees, they tend to grow vigorously once planted.

Winnowing: The act of separating seeds from lighter plant debris, such as chaff, often using wind or a gentle breeze to blow away unwanted materials.

ACKNOWLEDGEMENTS

To Ted, my constant companion in life and work, thank you for all you do.

To Rex, watching you grow up in this garden has been the greatest magic of all.

To my sister Imo, for reading the proofs with such love, detail, and care.

To Gemma, for bringing such thoughtful design to every page and tying it all together so beautifully.

To Harriet, for your generous edits, your patience, and your steady encouragement every step of the way, three and a bit years and we finally got it out into the world!

To Molly, my sweetest agent, thank you.

To Paris, my brilliant business partner, the reason this book ever made it to the page. Your work behind the scenes carries more than anyone knows.

And to Éva, your joy, your eye, your photographs, and your calm amid the chaos; this book is as much yours as it is mine. Thank you, endlessly.

Quadrille, Penguin Random House UK, One Embassy Gardens, 8 Viaduct Gardens, London SW11 7BW

Quadrille Publishing Limited is part of the Penguin Random House group of companies whose addresses can be found at global. penguinrandomhouse.com

Published by Quadrille in 2026

www.penguin.co.uk

A CIP catalogue record for this book is available from the British Library

ISBN 978 1 8378 3225 5
10 9 8 7 6 5 4 3 2 1

Managing Director Sarah Lavelle
Editorial Director Harriet Butt
Senior Designer Gemma Hayden
Photographer Éva Németh
Illustration Milli Proust
Head of Production Stephen Lang
Production Manager Sabeena Atchia

Colour reproduction by F1

Printed in China by C&C Offset Printing Co., Ltd.

The authorised representative in the EEA is Penguin Random House Ireland, Morrison Chambers, 32 Nassau Street, Dublin D02 YH68.

Penguin Random House is committed to a sustainable future for our business, our readers and our planet. This book is made from Forest Stewardship Council® certified paper.

ABOUT THE AUTHOR

MILLI PROUST lives and grows in West Sussex, UK. She has been cultivating and cropping cut flowers for designing with for coming up to a decade. She runs a busy floral design studio and cut flower seed line with her business partner Paris Alma under the name Alma Proust. She lives with her husband, two sighthounds, Jimmy and Stella and son Rex, who has just joined the family. Rex is already being taught the names of the plants and the trees in the hope that one day he'll join in on the growing. Milli Proust's debut book, *From Seed to Bloom (2020)*, was published by Quadrille.

www.milliproust.com | @milliproust